Simply the Best

Simply the Best:

29 Things Students Say the Best Teachers Do Around Relationships

By

Kelly E. Middleton

and

Elizabeth A. Petitt

AuthorHouse™
1663 Liberty Drive
Bloomington, IN 47403
www.authorhouse.com
Phone: 1-800-839-8640

First published by AuthorHouse 4/9/2010

ISBN: 978-1-4520-1004-5 (e)
ISBN: 978-1-4520-1003-8 (sc)

Library of Congress Control Number: 2010904740

Printed in the United States of America
Bloomington, Indiana

This book is printed on acid-free paper.

-Acknowledgements:

No achievement or accomplishment ever comes to fruition without the inspiration, encouragement, guidance and support of others. It is through the efforts of others, one is able to achieve goals and to pursue dreams. As educators, every day is a privilege and an opportunity to learn about and learn with our students. We have within our reach the opportunity to extend our reach to others. We have the ability to use our words to guide a student's educational journey. We have the ability to recognize students as individuals. We have the power to offer a positive image of the future and share a belief that all students can be successful. We have the responsibility of asking questions and listening as students inform our efforts and practices. This book is an acknowledgement of all those teachers and students who have helped us grow personally and professionally.

We would especially like to recognize and honor *all the staff* of Mason County Schools in Maysville, Kentucky. The adults are committed to excellence and do not define their job based on a list of responsibilities from a job description. Four years ago, Mason County teachers began conducting home visits. Each year, every student (preschool through grade twelve) is visited by his/her teacher prior to the beginning of school. These informal visits enable teachers to interact and build relationships with students and their families. Mason County teachers are committed to developing relationships with students while holding high expectations and communicating, "I believe in you!" There are countless random acts of kindness by staff members in an effort to address barriers to learning or barriers that prevent participation in school activities. Many of the activities listed in the last chapter are the brainchild of the creative and caring staff members in Mason County. Thank you not only for your ideas, but for your commitment and connection to students in your classroom. You are the difference-makers!

We would also like to thank all those individuals who assisted in the research, writing, and publishing of this book. To all the students who shared their realities, their beliefs, and their experiences, know your insights were invaluable. To all those who read the manuscript, commented, offered suggestions, and penned endorsements, know your input was used and we hold you in high esteem. To our families and friends, know we consider ourselves blessed because of your love and support.

Thanks to all those who share their expertise, their devotion to students, their passion for learning and their willingness to give of themselves on a daily basis. You are living a life of purpose and even though you may never know the extent of your influence, know students depend on you and see themselves through your eyes and through your words every day!

Contents

Introduction

Your success as an educator is more dependent on positive, caring, trustworthy relationships than on any skill, idea, tip or tool on effective teaching strategies.

-Eric Jensen

Introduction

*I've learned that people will forget what you said, people will forget
what you did, but people will never forget how you made them feel.*
-Maya Angelou

Traditionally in schools, our primary focus has been on academics and on the teaching act. Without question, these are essential aspects of schooling. However, there is a growing realization that teaching itself, in the absence of targeting learning, falls woefully inadequate in optimizing educational possibilities for all students. There is a second, but seldom articulated realization, that targeting learning in the absence of relationships truncates the opportunity for student success.

Maya Angelou's words are thought provoking. They remind us that our recollections are narrated by emotional overtones. How others make us feel creates a lasting impression that can be recalled vividly throughout one's lifetime. We may not remember all the elements in the periodic table, subject-verb agreement, or the Pythagorean theory. However, we will remember the relationship aspect. What type of connection did I have with my teacher? How did my teacher make me feel about my ability? Did my teacher instill a love for learning and an attitude that I could be successful? Was my school experience characterized by adults who knew the importance of relationships? Was I valued not only as a student, but as a person? People never forget how you made them feel.

Keep an Open Mind

We are so appreciative of all the teachers who day after day confront their realities with courage and determination, who work tirelessly to help students, who are there for their students when no one else is, and who often give beyond measure, without any expectation other than being "in the moment" and being there for their students. There are literally thousands of

2

teachers who refuse to give up on students. However, we are a prisoner of our own experiences. We become habituated to looking at school from our professional perspective. Inadvertently, we become insulated about what it means to be a student in our classrooms or in our schools.

The goal in school is success for each student. Henry Ford once shared, "If there is one secret to success, it lies in the ability to get the other person's point of view and see things from that person's angle, as well as your own." It is important to look at learning from the students' perspective, to consider their ideas and viewpoints. Education and learning experiences as seen through the eyes of the students offer valuable insights. Our role is simply to listen to what students have to say, without becoming defensive, and consider the merit of their ideas.

Looking at schools from the student angle, one could find a variety of experiences. Just as there are many inspiring stories about what happens in schools, there are also untold stories about what individual students experience not representative of what we want schools to be. Learning is often enhanced by non-examples of an idea or concept. Unfortunately, it is not difficult to find examples illustrating how the school experience can shortchange some students. In fact, it would almost be impossible to find a person unable to share a war story about his or her experience as a student, whether in a K-12 setting, in a post-secondary one or whether it is a public school or a private school. Typically, these war stories have nothing to do about the content. Generally, they revolve around the teacher-student interaction.

Following are three excerpts as shared by students about one of their most memorable experiences at schools. Be forewarned these are non-examples that attest to the power of the teacher-student relationship. These stories resulted in students not only feeling badly about themselves, but also how they perceived themselves as learners. Please read each of these from two perspectives. First, take the "angle" of the student and ask yourself, "What if I were this student? How might I react?" Secondly, take the angle of a teacher and ask yourself, "Could this or a similar situation happen in my school or district?

Jeremy

Jeremy was a high school student involved in a discussion with a teacher. They were engaged in a casual conversation about school, learning, and his status as a student athlete. Admittedly, he could occasionally need re-direction because classes and grades were not always at the top of his list. During the conversation, he unexpectedly reflected on his entire school experience, noting most his teachers were good, but there was one year he would never forget. This year was referred to as the year he had his "worst" teacher.

Jeremy painfully recalled that his father had died in third grade. He had been killed in a car accident. Upon returning to school, his teacher seemed frustrated with the entire class and unhappy to be there. However, he felt she lashed out at him. Because of his absence, this teacher asked for his homework. He did not have it. This was met by the teacher yelling at him and knocking over a desk. Extreme grief was compounded by humiliation and anger. Jeremy's family came to school the next day and asked for him to be placed in another classroom.

Thomas

A teacher shared an experience that continues to haunt him as a professional. He was asked to witness a discussion between one of his middle school colleagues and a student, who was experiencing some difficulty in class. The student was inattentive, not on task, and not engaged in a series of lessons. While in the hallway, this teacher asked, "What's wrong with you? If you keep this up, you are going to fail this class. Why are you not doing what you need to do? You have been in trouble all week. You don't even have enough pride about yourself to come to school clean. Don't you care about yourself or what you do? What's going on?

Immediately, the young man started to sob because of the humiliation he was feeling, humiliation as a student, humiliation as a person. The accusatory tone of the teacher and his sheer embarrassment resulted in no words, but continuing tears.

The teacher did not want to be a witness any longer. He walked away. Questions were fired at the student. Instead of a conversation which would have enabled him to keep his dignity, he felt attacked. His parents withdrew him from school the next day.

Sharon

Sharon was an undergraduate student at a university. She attended class every day, even on those days before a holiday. The teacher had students sign a roster on those days and promised extra credit. Even though it was a class where students were not penalized for their attendance, there were some students who showed up to class every day and asked questions. However, there were several who would only attend when tests were scheduled. The end of the semester came and the entire class showed up in the auditorium for the final.

The teacher sat on stage monitoring the exam. There were steps on both sides of the stage. Students quietly proceeded to either side of the stage and up the steps to turn their exams into the teacher. While Sharon was preparing to walk up the stairs on one side of the stage and turn in her exam, one of her classmates in front of her dropped his answer sheet. She picked it up and handed it to him as the teacher turned to that side of the stage. Sharon did not even know the name of that classmate.

Sharon and the young man were accused of cheating in front of the entire class. Each tried to share with the instructor what occurred but he didn't want to take the time to listen. The instructor refused to even compare the answer sheets. Sharon and the young man were humiliated in front of everyone else. Each was required to remain on stage with the professor until all the other students had completed the exam. Sharon was so upset that she had been accused of cheating, and that those in class who did not know her would assume she was not an honest person.

What are some of the words to describe the feelings you would associate with these stories if you were the student? In two of the three cases, students did not return to the same classroom or even the same school. As a teacher, do you think their experiences are atypical? Are we aware of what is being conveyed in some classrooms and schools? Are we aware of the fragile nature of relationships and how they impact learning? All three students probably had well-intentioned instructors who would never want to negatively impact students; but, they did. What was the message each one of these students walked away with about themselves, about their teachers, and about their schools? The number one fear of students in school is being publicly humiliated or embarrassed. How might these students characterize their experiences?

These are examples of what happens when we do not know our students, when we fail to look beyond our curricular roles and responsibilities, and when individuals are confronted with situations where we react before thinking. As professionals, we must become more deliberate about our interactions, more purposeful in our efforts to develop relationships, and more willing to incorporate the student perspective into the school milieu. By seeing school from the angle of the other person, as well as our own, the educational enterprise becomes more likely to result in positive outcomes for all.

Seeking to Understand

The goals of education are multi-faceted. We do not have illusions schools exist ostensibly to create learners who value themselves without the benefit of high expectations and academic knowledge. However, we do have a vision about the possibilities that exist to maximize learning experiences for students by establishing and utilizing relationships as the engine that drives rigor, that drives student achievement, and that ultimately drives the realization of personal and professional goals. There is a growing body of research which gives credence to this vision. Although a small slice of that research can be found in this book, there is a vacuum among educational literature contemplating the question, "What do the students say?"

Stephen Covey, author of the book, *The Seven Habits of Highly Effective People,* articulated a set of principles to enable individuals and organizations to be more productive. One of the habits has produced a mantra esteemed in many organizations. That mantra challenges us, "Seek first to understand." Everyone comprehends the significance of the statement, but living it is much more difficult. This book is our effort to seek understanding; to seek the views and perspectives of students. When asked, students have the ability to verbalize things making a difference to them as a person and as a learner in our schools. When asked, students have the ability to problem solve and offer solutions to problems occurring at school. When asked, students who regularly provide input feel more ownership in their schools. Amazingly, when asked about what the best teachers do in their classrooms that promote learning, they are able to identify practices in their own vernacular, ideas which are also found in professional literature with more esoteric descriptions. Students know what works.

The **STUDENT VOICE** is the impetus for this book. It is the predominant perspective sought and shared in the following chapters. These are shared as a way of informing us about our efforts in schools and as a guide for reflecting on our practices. After listening and talking with students, there were certain responses appearing multiple times in different discussion groups. This resulted in the identification of twenty-nine (29) things students say the best teachers do.

Two others nuances will aid your understanding about the organization and content of the book. First of all, as we contemplated relationships beyond a moral imperative or simply because it is the right thing to do, the question arose about the significance of relationships around the decisions educators make regarding curriculum, instruction, and assessment. What practices might educators identify related to curriculum, instruction, and assessment with relationships and personalization as the heart of our efforts? This led to the identification of concepts within each of these dimensions.

Secondly, the **RESEARCH VOICE** is offered as a way of explaining concepts for each of the dimensions presented. These concepts were not meant to be all-inclusive in terms of best practices in each of these areas, nor were the explanations meant to function as the primary guides for practice. The concepts were included in each dimension because they exemplify concepts which can be directly related to relationships, as well as concepts promoting student effort and involvement. They are key in leveraging relationships to maximize student success. The explanations provide readers with an overview of the significance of each of the concepts with professional literature and research lighting the way.

As you prepare to read and think your way through the following chapters, be cognizant that the first chapter initially asks you to contemplate how public schools are perceived. The term customer service is introduced and you are challenged to reflect on the question, "Who is the first customer?" Chapter one also invites you to adopt a student or parent perspective and think about what our customers value. The remainder of the chapter is devoted to underscoring the rationale for systemically addressing relationships within our schools. Twenty-four excerpts were compiled into a table from various professional sources and five realities were elucidated to answer the question, "Why focus on relationships?"

Chapters two through six examine relationships around five themes. These themes include: Relationships Around a Moral Imperative, Relationships Around Curriculum, Relationships Around Instruction, Relationships Around Assessment, and Relationships Around Recovery. These chapters incorporate graphic organizers as a way to visually depict elements from the research voice at the beginning of each chapter and as a point of comparison between the research and student voice near the end of the chapter. Readers will have a clear sense of how research supports consideration of key tenets for educational decision-making. Readers will also have a clear sense of what students say makes the best teacher within the dimension discussed in each chapter.

Chapter seven reconnects to the recurring theme of the power of relationships in schools and classrooms. The student voice is a valid one and should be heard as schools seek avenues for improvement efforts. The chapter concludes by challenging readers to see their students *in color,* and how that colored snapshot will impact our decisions, but most importantly our interactions with students.

Finally, chapter eight is a listing of ideas for teachers and schools. Eighty (80) ideas are explained that can be utilized on an individual teacher basis, as well as through school wide efforts when focusing on relationships and customer service. These ideas are an example of the caliber of practitioners as they find ways to make connections and develop positive relationships between the students, parents, and schools. There are also two self-assessment tools for individual teachers or schools to utilize. In one, ideas from the student voice are delineated for one to evaluate while the second one presents ideas about relationships stemming from the research voice that can be viewed from the classroom or school perspective.

One more feature will be evident as you read this book. Reflective practices should be the hallmark of our profession. At the end of chapters one through six, you are asked to reflect on your own experiences as a student around certain concepts. You are asked to share any AHA's that emerge related to classroom practices. These are entitled, *A Trip Down Memory Lane.* A second reflection is more from a teacher and school leader point of view. It asks you to contemplate elements within the research voice and within the student voice, denoting strengths and areas for potential growth for your school and for you, as an individual teacher.

Finally, please resist the temptation to dismiss ideas presented or to check them off under the guise of "We already do this." Our concept of doing this encompasses intentionality and planning. It could be evidenced by asking students, "Does this happen in your classroom?" "Does this happen at your school?" It is a mindset about how we interact with **all** students regardless of their socioeconomic status, regardless of their ethnicity and regardless of their abilities. Michael Fullan, educational author, researcher, and policy-maker makes the statement,

"You can borrow or steal a technique, but never a philosophy or culture" (Fullan, 2008, p. 16). It is our belief relationships shape the culture of a school. It is a culture you must create. It is a culture shaped by valuing students and their voices.

Chapter 1

Why Relationships?

For every one of us that succeeds, it's because there's somebody there to show you the way out. The light doesn't necessarily have to be in your family; for me it was teachers and school.

-Oprah Winfrey

Public schools – just hearing the phrase evokes visual images which could be accompanied by a host of emotionally charged words. Would most people convey a positive or negative reaction? First of all, consider the word public and how it is used. There are public restrooms, public housing, public healthcare, public transportation, and public pools. Generally, each of these endeavors is associated with the need to fill an existing void for needs and services. While many would assert it is better than not having anything at all, the general impression associated with anything run by the government or a bureaucracy is generally one of low expectations and the mindset that it's probably not very good because it offers a "one size fits all" approach to the issue. Everything is standardized and conceptualized around providing a common experience to a situation.

What about public schools? How would most people rate them? The answer would vary depending on an individual's experience in the world of school. School is one of those universal occurrences which may be defined more in terms of its diversity, rather than its commonality. Everyone's story may begin with, "Once upon a time." Unfortunately, every person's story does not end with, "…And they lived happily ever after." While one would never advocate that every person's story be the same, the opportunity for happy endings should be an expectation. The sad reality is some stories never get written.

What influences these stories of students in schools throughout the country? Success in schools can be attributed to a number of factors. Reviewing professional literature, one would discover enough ideas to wallpaper a room with practices associated with successful schools. Just think about it. Within seconds, educators can brainstorm twenty to thirty ideas including concepts such as leadership, aligned curricula, higher order thinking skills, relevance, rigor, differentiation, questioning, classroom management, deconstructing standards, technology, interventions, high expectations, assessment (formative, summative, common, diagnostic), data analysis, feedback, school culture, not to mention all the research based instructional strategies. It's a travesty schools often feel compelled to try to learn multiple concepts with the unrealistic expectation of immediate implementation. This implementation is expected to be accomplished with limited professional development, with little or no time provided for collaborative planning, with fidelity to the critical attributes of the concepts, and with consistency among all classrooms.

What is the result? Schools become obsessed with trying to find the "silver bullet" to help all students achieve. The goal is to "fix" the kids. Students are only seen from a content or academic perspective. Teachers end up trying to learn and juggle a multitude of "new" programs or approaches simultaneously. As a result, we often lose sight of the individual pupils and all the things happening in their lives which influence their ability to learn and succeed. Those who believe teachers should only focus on instruction, while sacrificing relationships, are embracing a premise that diminishes the nature of what constitutes good teaching.

One might make the argument that in the high stakes accountability environment where schools are bombarded with increasing expectations and sometimes judged as successes or failures based on one indicator, students can easily become invisible. Students become by-products of a system having the purest of motives, but one in which students seem to shrink a little each day due to pressure to by-pass the most important variable for success, getting to know the students and developing positive relationships. Students almost disappear from the school's landscape in terms of seeing them as individuals, observing their mannerisms and body language, noting changes, asking questions about their demeanor, or interacting with them informally about their interests beyond the school day. The construct of time and the myth that "positive relationships *already exist*" and are not as important as some of the other "stuff" impacting success on accountability measures, contributes to some dismissing the significance of making connections in schools. Unfortunately, this results in finding relationships and a multitude of other initiatives in the educational cemetery we shall call, *The Cemetery of the Tried and Abandoned.* Relationships are buried under the piles of things deemed as possessing more leverage for improving student achievement or for closing the achievement gaps, a practice with dire consequences for schools. In contemplating the question, what influences students' stories in school, one must be diligent to ensure each student's story includes meaningful teacher and student interaction. The stories of students in schools can have more positive plots resulting in happier endings (i.e. improved student achievement) when school improvement efforts systematically address the development of relationships and utilize these connections to establish high expectations.

Customer Service and Schools

Schools exist to educate. Educate comes from the word educare which means to nourish, rear or bring up. It is often associated with the Latin origin educere which means to draw forth. When we think about education from a broad perspective, with the idea of nourishing or even drawing forth associated with its etymology, how often do we think of the individual nature of the enterprise as a primary determinant as opposed to the outcome we are seeking? We cannot educate without considering the "who" – Who are the students we teach? Embracing this belief translates into embracing the concepts of customer service and an intentional focus on relationships in schools. Even though customer service is a term that is borrowed from the business world, examining schools and education from a customer service perspective provides a unique approach for returning to the fundamental purpose most educators chose teaching as a profession – to make a difference.

14

Customer service is a standard in the business world measured by making customers feel important, valued, and insuring every effort is made to maximize their experience by anticipating and addressing their needs. For schools, the expectation may exceed the ideas inherent in the Golden Rule: treating others like we would want to be treated. What would happen in schools if everyone made a commitment to treat the "customer" better than we would want to be treated? How might that transform schools?

The first step for schools is the realization, "Yes, we do have customers!" Even though some would assert this statement is subject to debate within the educational arena, schools must realize that parents have a choice about who will partner with them in the education of their child. For schools, customer service reaches beyond the brief encounters typically associated with customer service in the business world. It is not about a benign experience related to the purchase of a product, the type of service or quality of food while dining in a restaurant, nor from the solicitation of one's reactions to services provided. The type of customer service needed in schools shatters the typical customer service ideas in the business world because we are dealing with people's children. Customer service in schools is not limited to intermittent encounters or exchanges. Schools have customers with whom we interact and influence on a daily basis. Schools are charged with the responsibility of promoting growth in academic, social, and emotional realms while appreciating the uniqueness of each student.

Once schools have embraced the belief they are in the customer service business, the next step in the process is responding to the question, "Who are our customers and why?" If you were asked to respond to this question, how would you answer? Is it the staff, the students, the parents, or the community? Answering this question within educational endeavors is often more dicey than the business world. One could make various arguments about, "Who is the customer?" Some might assert school is a reflection of the community and the taxpayers who invest in the future of that community. Others might lobby that parents are the main customers as the primary decision-makers related to what occurs in their household, as well as being able to choose where their child will attend school. What about the students? Ultimately, one must consider the individuals walking through the doors to our schools and classrooms day after day – the students. Are they not the main customers?

Determining who constitutes the first customers is an important initial step for schools. Two caveats should be noted prior to this dialogue. The first caveat underscores one of the customer service principles identified in the bo*ok, Who Cares, Improving Public Schools Through Relationships and Customer Service* (Middleton & Petitt, 2007). If there is an expectation teachers will provide good customer service to others, administrative personnel must model good customer service practices to their staff. Secondly, public schools often have a reputation for being more adult centered than student centered. Administrators must treat staff members with respect, seek their input, provide them with appropriate resources and training and develop leadership capacity among them. We are a part of a team working collectively to meet the needs of individual students. However, when there are competing interests, which sometimes exist in schools, it is critical schools ground themselves with the knowledge that students are the "first" customers. If we fail to acknowledge students with this distinction, we may one day find the demand for our expertise and services are not needed, that our retirement systems have been dismantled, and that our customers have made other choices about their education and who will partner with them in that process.

As one contemplates the idea of schools being in the customer service business and as we determine who the main customers are, then we must think about schools from the customer perspective. How would our customers rate our schools in terms of quality of the product – the success of individual students in schools? How would they evaluate their interaction and communication with schools? When perusing the customer service statistics and reviewing articles related to customer satisfaction, it's alarming to view how most customers in the business world rate their customer service experiences. John R. Dijulius III (2008) authored the book, *What's the Secret? To Providing a World-Class Customer Service Experience.* After conducting in-depth research of various businesses, he identified trends in the levels of customer service. Based on his research, DiJulius concluded, "79 percent of the companies provide a level of customer service which is average at best" with 41% of (those) companies being ranked as delivering unacceptable or below average levels of customer service" (p. 5). Consideration of this trend from a public education perspective generates three questions which beg to be asked:

1. How might the customers of schools rate their performance?

2. How would that compare to the trends DiJulius identified?

The final question focuses on point of view.

3. How would those who work in public schools rate the service they provide to their customers?

One cannot help but wonder if a discrepancy would exist between the two perspectives. If a discrepancy occurred, it would be interesting to ascertain if it paralleled the pattern that emerged from the research of Bain and Company who surveyed 362 companies and found while eighty (80) percent of companies believed they provided superior service, only eight (8) percent of their customers were in agreement (DiJulius, 2008, p. 6).

Assume the role of a student or parent at your school. Think about the practices the school engages in based on our history and use of the platitude, "This is the way we've always done it." Is that history rich with stories about customer-friendly practices or are the stories more indicative of conducting the business of school in the absence of knowledge about the customers and their concerns? DiJulius (2008) shares a quote from Jack Mackey, vice president of Service Management Group emphasizing the importance of how people are treated. "You can say what you want about who you (think you) are, but people believe what they experience" (p. 5). What is the customer "experience" at your school? Do students think the teachers believe in them or does a "gotcha" mentality exist where students are scrutinized at a level the adults in that school would find uncomfortable? Is there an unforgiving atmosphere where many often relish in finding what students do wrong as opposed to celebrating what students do right? If roles were exchanged, *could you survive as a student in your school or classroom?* Think about the following.

	Your cell phone vibrates during class and you thought it was on silent. A lecture follows about school policy and disrespect. The phone is confiscated and your parents must find a time to come to school and pick it up from the office.
	You turn in all your homework on time with everything complete. You always get it back with just a check on it.
	You are sick and out of school for a week. No one calls to check on you. When you return to school, you are asked for all your work in one class by the next day.
	No adult smiles as you enter the class, and hardly anyone at school calls you by name.
	You don't understand something in school and the teacher goes on with the content, stating, "Why don't you listen? Maybe you don't belong in my class and need to be moved to a remedial class."
	There's a knock on the classroom door. You are taking a test in this class. You are informed that your grandmother has died. The teacher asks you to finish the test before you leave.
	You must move to a different classroom. Upon entering, the teacher rolls her eyes announcing, "I don't have enough chairs and I'm already at capacity."

How would you feel if you were asked to trade places? Do you feel valued? These are just a few real-life examples shared by students. Does your perspective change when you think about your experience as a student?

Schools are a reflection of their values. In some educational literature, this phenomenon is known as the hidden curriculum. "The messages of hidden curriculum usually deal with attitudes, values, beliefs, and behavior" and can be conveyed directly or indirectly (Cornbleth, 2009, p. 1), Words can exist in mission statements asserting a belief in helping all students reach their potential enabling them to become productive members of the community. The question becomes, "Do the actions within schools mirror the mission posted on school walls?" Do we realize helping students reach their potential is predicated on knowing our students and developing positive relationships with students and their families? Would our customers communicate to us that schools value relationships and the individuality of students? Educators and school personnel must reflect on the values communicated through our words and actions. The hidden curriculum, particularly the cultural aspects of it, is just as important as the written curriculum and the stated messages of the school. One can only hope the hidden curriculum doesn't contradict the mission statements that are proudly displayed in the halls of our schools. We must embrace the idea that our customers are always judging our efforts through our interactions with them. We must embrace the perspective of looking at schools from the eyes of the students and parents. We must embrace the individual nature of the process of education, contemplating what students value, and being purposeful in how we interact. We must not lose sight of our first customers lest we lose the opportunity to maximize the educational experiences, achievement, and opportunities of our students.

What Do Our Customers Value?

Before considering what is valued by our customers, imagine ourselves on the outside peering through the window of school, observing what is emphasized. What might be identified as school priorities? If we were to offer an objective commentary about what schools value, would it be relationships and customer service, or would it be high stakes accountability efforts? Would one witness students being bombarded with a barrage of standardized assessments? There is evidence as some parents peer through that window; they would characterize their view being dominated by too much testing. As a result they are opting out of the public school system. Everything is a matter of perspective, and before contemplating what our customers value, one must at least take a few minutes and think about what would be the current descriptors used to describe what schools esteem. One cannot help but wonder how that compares with what is significant to the students, our first customers.

As one reflects about these customers, often we assume the demands would be so great; one could not possibly implement a customer service focus because there would be no way of meeting the expectations. When interviewing students, it is disconcerting to learn their expectations about relationships in schools are minimal. The bar is not set high, as one might anticipate, but one that is set so low by students; it would be achievable without the need for additional funds or resources. The following story illustrates this idea.

Janine

Janine was a young lady whose life circumstances were so dire that it caused her to catch a train to escape a life few could imagine surviving. Amtrak officials notified local authorities of their suspicion that a young lady was a runaway from one of the northeastern states. After various legal protocols, Janine was placed in a local home.

Janine enrolled as a senior in the high school and upon conversing with her, one could surmise she was articulate, talented, and had probably experienced some of life's more difficult challenges. As a discussion ensued about Janine's experience at her previous school, the question was asked, "Was there one adult or teacher you connected with at your other high school?" The immediate response was no but after thinking for a moment, Janine revised her answer by sharing, "Well, maybe there was one teacher."

As the conversation continued Janine shared that her math teacher was the one teacher she felt cared about her succeeding. When prompted to share why she thought this teacher cared, without pausing to think she volunteered, "He smiled at me and greeted me each day as I entered class. He also took the time to try to help me or made sure I had a tutor after school when I was having trouble with certain math concepts."

As an educator listening to this young woman reflecting on her experience as a student at her previous school and her adjustment as a new student in our district, there was a sense of shame and embarrassment that something as simple as a smile and greeting had made such a difference in a student's life. Someone who acknowledged a student's name, smiled, and periodically offered additional academic support– these behaviors and expectations seemed so low. It's a sad indictment of the education profession if staff members are unable to meet these expectations. However, it was also reassuring as she made eye contact and volunteered, "It's very different here! Here everyone has been nice and seems to care. From my homeroom teacher to other students, people have made me feel welcome."

When we finished talking with Janine, we made an unannounced visit to her homeroom teacher where we learned that Mr. Hawkins already knew Janine had an interest in art and made sure she was able to enroll in an upper level art class. He had also contacted other teachers to ensure Janine was making a smooth transition. Knowing our teachers go the extra mile for students is a tribute to educators who know who the main customers are and what a difference they make in the lives of their students. (Thanks to all those in the profession who share that sense of purpose and drive to help all students be successful!)

Think about Janine's experience, her perspective, her words. Was Janine's description of what she valued an anomaly? The resounding answer to that question is, "No!" Based on extensive interviews with students in a variety of settings at all levels, students are able to verbalize what good teachers say and do. A list of those practices and ideas will be presented later. Suffice is to say, Janine's response offers educators with insights about the importance of their interactions with students and conveys the power of the conventional wisdom, "It's the little things that matter."

Why Should I Care About Customer Service?

Customer service and public schools – these two concepts are usually not viewed in a relational manner. Those involved in the education profession have many competing interests and it's not unusual for one to verbalize, "Why should I focus on customer service? What's in it for me?" This is a fair question because we are always seeking relevance and determining priorities within our personal and professional lives. There is a litany of ideas which could be generated in response to these inquiries. The following table takes a philosophical approach in providing one response. It delineates ideas from research and national experts with diverse backgrounds and ideologies. As you peruse the twenty-four views shared, think about what your school or classroom looks like and sounds like in relation to the ideas presented.

A Word from a Few of the Experts
Why relationships deserve an intentional focus in schools....

No significant learning occurs without a significant relationship.

-Dr. James Comer

The quality of relationships teachers have with their students is the keystone to effective classroom management and perhaps even the entirety of teaching.

-Robert Marzano

The primary motivator of whether kids in poverty will learn is whether they like the teacher. It's that relationship. It comes down to two things: you've got to teach them how to live in a paper world, and you have to have a relationship of respect with them.

-Ruby Payne

....the most important element in motivating students to want to achieve at high standards: the quality of relationships with their teachers. It has always been true that students tend to learn very little from teachers who they feel are not respectful toward them. They may feel goaded into doing the minimum by a teacher who uses fear and intimidation, but they will never do their best even in subjects they enjoy. And for today's students, who often have little contact with their parents or other adults, relationships with caring, respectful teachers have become even more important.

-Tony Wagner, Robert. Kegan,, et al. (2006, p. 42)

Teacher caring and supportive interpersonal relationships have been linked to increased student learning, greater school satisfaction, and more positive academic values and attitudes toward school.

-Adena Klem and James Connell (2004, p. 62)

Know your students. Establish expectations that all students will become connected with a caring adult at school. When schools place a priority on educators and staff developing positive relationships with students, negative behavior and dropout rates rapidly diminish.

-Robert Barr & William Parrett

Programs don't change kids, relationships do ... nothing matters more to a child than a one-to-one steady relationship with an adult who cares about that child.

-William E. Milliken (2007)

We must never make people our projects. People need relationships. From the relationships built, we can better understand the needs and then consider how best to work with our new friends to remedy those needs...The student in the classroom is often not just struggling to learn the particular academic subject being studied. There may be physical and emotional battles. The family situation may be a mess. There may be nutritional issues or sleep deprivation. The student may have financial and transportation worries. When the educator considers the whole person there may be more patience and a greater motivation to teach to the student.

-Nora Stanger (2003)

African-American students care what school personnel want for them and need to know that school staff care about them and their futures.

-George Wimberly (2002)

Literature points to a strong link between positive nurturing interpersonal relationships between teachers and students as an important ingredient in the recipe for student success.

-Mark Weber (2007)

Relationships (students feeling connected to their school) have the ability of playing the most significant role in student development.
<div align="right">-Jack O'Connell California State Superintendent of Public Instruction</div>
All students need to know that at least one adult in the school continually cares about them and their future after high school...Adults who encourage students, monitor academic progress and social development, and have a general interest in students' futures can turn educational expectations into realistic goal.
<div align="right">-George Wimberly (2002)</div>
Human beings of all ages are happiest and able to deploy their talents to best advantage when they experience trusted others standing behind them.
<div align="right">-John Bowlby (1989, pp 124-125)</div>
Every child requires someone in his or her life who is absolutely crazy about them.
<div align="right">-Urie Bronfenbrenner (1991, p. 2)</div>
Learning requires caring. The more students believe that their school community cares about them and meets their needs, the more likely they are to feel attached to that community, to thrive academically, socially, and emotionally.
<div align="right">-Kimberly Schonert-Reichl (2006)</div>
Positive teacher-student relationships lead to higher academic motivation and academic success as well as increased student social emotional skills, such as caring, empathy and social responsibility.
<div align="right">Robert Roeser, Carol Midgley, & Tom Urdan (1996, p. 10); Kathryn Wentzel (2003)</div>
Students attending urban, suburban or rural high schools; students who struggle academically; and students who take advanced courses all say the one thing that makes the greatest difference in their learning is the quality of their relationships with their teachers. They want teachers who care about teaching and who are challenging, competent, of course, but what they talk about most often is how they are treated by their teachers. Does the teacher see them as individuals, rather than just faces in the crowd? Does the teacher try to know and understand what students may be dealing with at home or in their neighborhood? To what extent does a teacher go out of his or her way to ensure that all students are learning versus just plowing through the chapters? Or does the teacher only pay attention to the "smart" kids? It is increasingly clear to us that, although many of today's students may have diminished fear and respect for formal authority, they have an increased need to connect with adults who can guide and coach them in school and in life (pp 42-43).
<div align="right">-Tony Wagner, Robert Kegan, et al. (2006, pp 42-43)</div>
...the twin messages of teaching should never be teased apart: 'I care about you. And I care about your learning'.
<div align="right">-Marge Scherer (2008, p. 7)</div>
But the students who seemingly deserve the most punitive consequences we can muster are actually the ones who need a positive personal connection with their teacher.
<div align="right">-Rick Smith & Mary Lambert,(2008, p. 19)</div>
When students know that you believe in them, they will interpret even harsh-sounding comments as statements of care from someone who has their best interests at heart. As one student commented, "She's mean out of the kindness of her heart" ....these teachers insist on two things: **students treat the teacher and one another respectfully* **complete academic tasks necessary for successful futures*
<div align="right">-Elizabeth Bondy & Dorene Ross (2008, pp. 54-58)</div>

Principal of Woodstock High School in Illinois, Cory Tofoya: *It's all about expectations and relationships. ..The biggest impact on improved student behavior has been our improved relationships among teachers, administrators and students. We learn the name of every student and we really care about them .* <div align="right">-Douglas Reeves (2008, p. 86)</div>
A better way to reach students is to proactively cultivate "intentionally inviting" practices that welcome all students into the culture of learning. <div align="right">-Sue Zapf (2008, p. 68)</div>
We signal to students from the moment they step into school whether they belong or whether we see them as trespassers. <div align="right">-Linda Christensen (2008, p. 62)</div>
What made you stick it out when others just like you quit? *We posed this question to individual students who were succeeding despite the odds. In every case, the students said they had an important connection to school in some way, usually through a significant relationship with an adult on the staff.* <div align="right">-Christopher Hill (2009, p. 18)</div>

This sampling of ideas from educational literature and from various perspectives suggests schools need to be more intentional in their efforts at establishing positive relationships in schools. If this table of research and practitioner snapshots are not compelling enough to answer the question, "Why relationships?", then perhaps one of the following five realities will enable school staff to understand the significance of focusing on relationships in schools.

Reality #1: School Choice is a Growing Concern for Public School Teachers

The school choice movement is gaining momentum as evidenced by information from the U.S. Department of Education. Since 1999, the number of homeschool students has increased by 56.6% (Bielick, 2008). There continues to be more choice-friendly legislation in all states. In many states, this is leading to fewer resources for public schools, as well as recommendations for changes in retirement and health care benefits for teachers.

Reality #2: A Teacher & Student Disconnect Exists in Many Schools

More students are feeling disenfranchised from schools. Even though the teacher and student relationship should be a priority in schools, there is an obvious disconnect between teachers and students in many schools. More than half of 414,243 students surveyed by Quaglia Institute (2008) say teachers do not care about their problems or feelings. Approximately half (48%) of the students felt teachers cared about them as individuals and forty-nine percent (49%) of the students shared they enjoyed being at school. (p. 18). Could there be a correlation between enjoying being at school and someone caring about students?

Reality #3: Relationships Play Important Role in Reducing Achievement Gaps

In closing the gap research and literature, a common thread emerges as a keystone for reducing gaps between learning subgroups. That common thread is a focus on relationships in schools. Students from poverty and diverse cultures, students who are struggling academically respond to educators who demonstrate they care about students as individuals. The relationship is at the heart of making progress toward elimination of gaps among various populations in school.

Reality #4: Impact of Classroom Teacher on Learning is Key in Student Achievement

More and more research continues to identify the classroom teacher as the single best influence on student achievement and the best form of intervention. In an article where Kati Haycock (1998), president of the Education Trust shares findings with United States Representatives, she referenced research from William L. Sanders at the University of Tennessee. This research offered compelling outcomes on the impact of the teacher. "In examining data in the state of Tennessee, he found that low achieving students gained about 14 points each year on the state test when taught by the least effective teachers, but gained more than 53 points when taught by the most effective teachers….High achieving students only gained about 2 points when taught by a low-effectiveness teacher, but more than 25 points a year under the guidance of top teachers" (n.p.). Quality teachers develop quality relationships with their students. Effective teachers not only have good verbal skills and great understanding of their content, they hold high expectations and work with students to ensure progress and success in the classroom.

Reality #5: Interactions Have Direct Influence on Student Learning

Based on 11,000 statistical findings over a fifty year period, Wang, Haertel, and Walberg (1994) synthesize it is not the indirect factors such as organizational structures and policies from the state, the district or the school having the greatest impact on student learning. It is not even parental involvement policies. Factors influencing student achievement are predicated primarily on the teacher student relationship. In fact, this analysis states the most significant influence on student learning is direct influence which is described as "…the amount of time a teacher spends on a topic and the quality of the social interaction a teacher has with their students" (p. 74). How often in our schools do we identify expectations related to those interactions?

One cannot assume that relationships will automatically develop in educational endeavors. Schools would benefit greatly by frontloading educational efforts with a concentrated focus on relationships. Robert Marzano (2007), author of the book, *The Art and Science of Teaching* asks the question, "What will I do to establish and maintain effective relationships with students?" (p. 149). He does not ask *if* we should do it. Marzano challenges those within the profession about *how* they will establish and maintain relationships; yet, how much planning and effort is systematically devoted to these efforts? In fact, one might observe conversations about relationships in school are conspicuously absent in the dialogue on school improvement efforts. If one reviewed most school and district plans, the alarming conclusion might be the absence of any teacher and student interactions being systematically addressed. This is an area whose absence in pre-service preparation and in school improvement efforts are seldom explored, discussed or addressed in terms of what these relationships are, why they are important, and how to build and promote them as an avenue to enhance student achievement.

Consider the Possibilities

The spectrum of relationship efforts begins by peering through the prism of possibilities. This prism of possibilities begins with initial efforts in relationship building and making connections and extends to the concept of personalization in educational experiences. Some schools are making tremendous gains through their incorporation of relationship building and personalization efforts. Linda Darling Hammond and Diane Friedlaender, researchers and associates of the School Redesign Network, assert schools can change their organizational structures to provide more support for students who are typically not successful in the traditional system. In their "successful by design" premise, one of the linchpins was personalization. Although rigorous and relevant curriculum characterized by professional collaboration were key design features as well, a concept that truly distinguished five California high schools who were more successful with poor or minority students from their counterparts focused on personalization. A philosophical underpinning of personalization was depicted as someone who takes ownership of students by refusing to give up, by fostering long-term relationships, by insuring students receive academic and personal support, and by "tailoring instruction to students' strengths, needs, experiences, and interests" (Darling-Hammond and Friedlaender,

2008, p. 16). Students respond to teachers who know who they are, who interact with them, and who communicate high expectations and a belief in the student's ability to be successful. In order to help students find their niche, schools and teachers must know the students. Consider the possibilities for you and your school.

Relationships: A Pillar for School Improvement

Regrettably, some educators are impervious to the vital role relationships play in schools and in student achievement. We can no longer afford to assume that relationships and making connections with students already exist as they should in the schoolhouse. We can no longer assume that relationships will be like a phoenix and "rise from the ashes" of instruction. Therefore, in order to understand the role of relationships and to pursue them with a sense of urgency and intentionality, it is incumbent to provide those who dismiss their significance or even to those who are reserving judgment, that a systematic focus on relationships is one of the first pillars we must construct in school improvement efforts. It is with these ideas in mind that the following chapters were developed. Just as a reminder, recall that each of the next five chapters is organized into two distinct sections.

One section is the **research voice** which seeks to identify some of the major tenets related to moral imperative, to curriculum, to instruction, to assessment, and to recovery. If one were to contemplate relationships around these dimensions, what are some of the aspects that might emerge as important elements to consider within that domain? A list has been generated around each of these dimensions. Educational literature is utilized to describe these practices, especially in the context of promoting academic success for students. As stated in the introduction, it is not the intent to provide a detailed review of all the research and professional literature linking relationships to each of these dimensions. It is a goal to illustrate how relationships weave in and out of these educational concepts and practices, as well as how students are impacted by the decision-making of schools and teachers within these domains.

The second section is the **student voice.** These ideas were collected by listening to students in focus groups from elementary, middle and high schools over the past five years and by consulting additional sources describing characteristics students ascribed to what they considered the best teachers. Students articulated a myriad of practices. However, some ideas were recurrent themes in student conversations. As a result, twenty-nine practices have been delineated to represent the student voice. Many of these practices have *subtle* differences based on the repetition of the idea from student to student and the descriptors and examples students used to share their experiences and analysis of what the best teachers do. The twenty-nine ideas from the student voice could have been collapsed into a broader framework with fewer ideas; however, the power of the student voice is reflecting on the presence or absence of each of the ideas in schools. Each behavior or action on the part of the teacher was significant to students as they discussed what the best teachers do. These are categorized into the five domains on the basis of what was a good fit between the practice and the domain category.

By comparing the research voice and the student voice, one begins to envision why relationships and making connections are important pillars in school improvement. They allow educators to create an educational environment and experiences mirroring practices that students identify as what the best teachers do. In the book, *The Six Secrets of Change,* the author shares the work of Henry Mitzberg who focused on the importance of the context of ideas and theories. Mitzberg offers a conclusion about learning. He asserts, "Learning is not doing; it is reflecting on doing" (Fullan, 2008, p. 5). Assume the role of learner as you turn the following pages. Most importantly, reflect on what you or your school is doing or should be doing as it relates to customer service and relationships.

Reflection

A Trip Down Memory Lane

Take a few moments and reflect on your experience as a student in a formalized setting. This can be at any educational level from elementary school through college.

Think about a teacher who made a profound impact on your life. Who was it and what attributes about this teacher or professor were especially meaningful for you? List those attributes below.

Think about a teacher or classroom where you felt frustrated as a learner. What caused this frustration? List those attributes below.

Think and Predict

As you think about the student voice and the teacher-student relationship, share four or five ideas you think students might identify as being important to them.

Read on to see how your experience as a student compares to the student voice ideas in the following chapters.

Chapter 2

Relationships Around
A Moral Imperative:
It's The Right Thing to Do

We are most likely to give our best to those we love and respect. I think back to my days in school, and I remember loving some teachers and having others who left me cold. I know that I always did my best for the teachers I liked and for the others I did only what was needed to get a grade.

-John Maxwell
(Maxwell & Parrott, 2005, p. 69)

Relationships Around A Moral Imperative Research Voice

A report issued by the 2003 Commission on Children at Risk which was comprised of a list of distinguished professionals surmised, "Humans are hardwired to connect with others" (Cowan, 2008, p. 1). The statistics in the study attested to the increasing incidence of children suffering from mental, physical and behavioral disorders. The commission deemed it a crisis. If the need to be connected and feel connected is a biological function, and if, as the study suggests, large and growing numbers of children are failing to flourish, how might schools bridge the gap that enables students to feel connected to the school community? There must be an intentional and purposeful pursuit of connections in schools. This results in not only fulfilling biological needs, but also in setting the stage for educational success.

As professionals, we must recognize the need for systematically addressing relationship efforts in schools. We must also make a commitment to taking the time, devoting the resources, and sharing this as an expectation of professionals within our field. Caring is one of the most important dispositions of not only teachers, but who we are as humans. Cognizance of the research, as well as insights from students, necessitates this element be present in schools. One would like to believe that educators would embrace the concept based on its own merit. We must start asking questions about what types of relationships exist in our schools and then begin the process of cultivating good teacher-student relationships, realizing it takes time, effort, patience and planning.

A rationale for the impact of relationships begins with the knowledge that schools work with individuals. It's a people business. Therefore, an intentional focus on relationships in schools begins with the belief that it is a moral imperative to learn about and celebrate the individuals who comprise classrooms of students throughout public schools everywhere. The central idea is capitalizing on the concept: *Who is this student as a person?*

Research encompassing relationships around a moral imperative is a theme which appears in a variety of professional literature. Many of these ideas were presented in the table in chapter one and underscores their significance in schools. In addressing relationships based on the merit of the idea itself, one is engaging in behaviors forming the foundation for establishing a bond that is a prerequisite for meaningful interactions between the teacher and the student. John Maxwell, author of multiple books on leadership believes we are most likely to give our best to those we love and respect. Are schools explicitly engaging in building relationship bridges? All students need and seek this type of connection with the teacher. However, it is critical among some populations of students and in developing resilience in young people. Bonnie Benard (2003) makes the following observation:

> A common finding in resilience research is the power of a teacher – often without realizing it – to tip the scale from risk to resilience…Among the most frequently encountered positive role models in the lives of the children…outside of the family circle, was a favorite teacher. For the resilient youngster, a special teacher was not just an instructor for academic skills but also a confidant and positive model for personal identification (p. 117).

We must remember we are not just teachers; we are individuals who wield influence in the lives of students. Whether that influence will be positive or negative basically hinges on the type and quality of the relationship with the teacher.

Dunsworth and Billings (2009) identify effectiveness indicators in high performing schools. They cite research from Brewster and Railsback (2003) underscoring why schools must be explicit in cultivating connections in schools: "…the quality of relationships within a school community makes a difference…while trust alone does not guarantee success, schools with little or no trust have almost no chance of improving" (p. 151). Students listen to every word and watch every act to ascertain if there is congruence between the message and how they are treated. They are evaluating the authenticity of our actions and are attempting to identity what Brewster and Railsback delineated as five components of trusting relationships: benevolence, reliability, competence, honesty and openness. The Learning First Alliance appraisal not only succinctly captures this idea, but is also in agreement with what a number of our customers share, "Students often remember how adults behave more than what they say" (Dunsworth & Billings, 2009, p. 147). Students feeling connected to schools is one of the initial goals schools should embrace when contemplating relationships in school improvement efforts. "There is strong empirical evidence that school connectedness contributes to a variety of important positive educational outcomes including increases in motivation, classroom engagement, attendance, academic achievement, and school completion rates" (Dunsworth & Billings, 2009, p. 128). It is important to take the first step and that step is planned around answering the question, "Who is this student as a person?" This can be addressed in a variety of ways including the six identified in the graphic organizer. To guide one's efforts in this area, the following questions under each subtopic may be helpful.

Knowing the student

- *What does the student enjoy doing? How does he/she spend free time?*
- *What barriers or obstacles are present that might impact impede progress?*
- *What is their favorite subject in school and why?*
- *How does the student feel about school? Why?*
- *What is this student's situation or story?*
- *Do we interact and see this student as an individual?*

Having high expectations and creating a culture of success

- *Do students know you believe in them?*
- *Do you work collaboratively with students to establish learning goals?*
- *Is effort valued and do all students have access to rigorous curriculum options?*
- *How do you assist students if they are experiencing difficulty learning a concept?*
- *What are the support mechanisms in place for the student at home and at school?*

Developing mutual trust and respect

- *Do the students know who you are as a person?*
- *Do you clearly communicate your expectations?*
- *Are you consistent in your interactions with all students?*
- *Do students feel safe and supported?*
- *Do you maintain confidentiality?*
- *Do you protect the dignity of each student, ensuring they are never embarrassed or humiliated in your presence?*
- *Do students believe they can count on you?*
- *Do you lead by example?*
- *Do you listen to students?*

Showing we care

- *Do you smile at students and acknowledge them whenever you see them?*
- *Do you use the students' names during your interaction with them?*
- *Do you call or check on students when they are absent from school?*
- *Are you genuine in your interactions with students?*
- *When you interact with students, are you "in the moment" mentally and emotionally there with students?*

Encouraging involvement in extracurriculars

- *Do you know what your students are involved in and what their gifts are?*
- *Do you make students aware of opportunities to showcase their interests and abilities?*
- *Do you attend special events in the lives of students (church performances, meets, ballgames, etc)?*
- *Do you help students overcome obstacles that might inhibit or prevent them from participating in extracurricular activities?*

Personalizing the learning environment

- *Is there an atmosphere in the classroom that conveys this is "our" classroom, as opposed to "your" classroom?*
- *Are examples of student work displayed?*
- *Are names and pictures of students used in displays?*
- *Are students provided with choice in your school or classroom?*
- *Do you recognize students for their success or their progress (and when possible, in ways that are meaningful to them)?*

These sample questions are meant to serve as guideposts to spur thinking; directing one toward intentionally forging relationships with students. Caring relationships are vital to the learning process. "Students report that caring relationships characterized by unwavering teacher access, support and pressure are the most powerful force in getting them to achieve at higher levels and graduate" (Ancess, 2008, p. 49). Getting to know the student as a person is a concept that should serve as the building block of all other connection efforts. Bondy and Ross (2008) discuss the duality of roles the teacher has describing the teacher as "warm demander." Students offered this piece of advice for teachers: "Remind us often you expect our best, encourage our efforts even if we are having trouble, give helpful feedback and expect us to review…don't compare us to other students and stick with us" (p. 56).

Relationships are not just a kindergarten through twelfth grade concern. They are an aspect extending beyond the boundaries of high school as students learn to navigate post-secondary opportunities and experiences. Although many colleges and universities often give the cold shoulder to the concept of making connections with their students and view their responsibilities exclusively as the dissemination and acquisition of knowledge as students pursue degrees, there are some colleges and universities who recognize high academic standards should be accompanied by making connections with their students.

Dr. William Crouch, president of Georgetown College in Kentucky, makes a personal connection by inviting all incoming students to his home on campus, making sure he shakes the hand of each student. He also shares with students if they pass his residence and the porch light is on, they are welcome to come in and talk about any issue. One way the administration of Georgetown College emphasizes the importance of making connections with students is through price adjustments made for lunches. If faculty members eat with the students, they receive a discount on their lunches. Some faculty members even report they visit the dorm to have a face-to-face conversation if a student is not attending class.

Dr. Brian Nichols, a dean at East Texas Baptist University gave a presentation in Chicago, Illinois entitled, "Improving Academic Performance through the Enhancement of Teacher/Student Relationships: The Relationship Teaching Mode". He noted, "A vehicle that contributes to optimum student learning is the ability to develop the proper relationship with students, a relationship that becomes a motivator for those involved in the learning experience" (Nichols, 2005, n.p.). Dean Nichols identified twelve contributors with multiple examples for each depicting relationship teaching. The contributors included such categories as promoting academic rigor, showing a personal interest in students, offering optional student assignments, and assisting students with community involvement. These are two examples illustrating the increasing number of post-secondary institutions addressing the significance of relationships. They are cognizant that students have choices and that the market share for on-line education is growing at staggering rates, ultimately impacting the bottom-line. They are also cognizant that post-secondary institutions have a responsibility to the individuals who matriculate through their doors beyond offering rigorous courses.

Relationships in schools can be difference-makers. From academic achievement to the fulfillment of social and emotional goals, research is replete with evidence attesting to the impact of positive relationships in schools. The power of connections is manifested in one-to-one interactions that occur on a daily basis. As educators, we often react to only what we can see. Our ability to look beyond the surface and understand the magnitude of our words and actions as we interact with students is critical to our success in schools. The impact is one which parallels watching a pebble skipping across the surface of water and then observing how ripples emerge from beneath the surface. It's always amazing to note how the force of one pebble reverberates even when it is no longer visible. This is the image one should envision when thinking how our words and actions are internalized by students.

Students Speak: What Our Customers Say

"Build it and they will come." This familiar line from the movie, *Field of Dreams* could be revised to say, "Ask them and they will tell you!" as the basis for looking at practices in schools and how they align with our customers' needs. As the first customer, students are able to effectively articulate the behaviors and actions of effective teachers which enable them to experience success in the classroom. After interviewing hundreds of students, as well as reading comments from various studies and authors, one is able to see patterns emerge from student responses. A majority of their comments hinge directly on the basic relationship of the teacher with the student and vice versa. When one thinks about an intentional focus on developing relationships with students, the words of the students resonate with clarity and a profound desire for adults viewing students on a human and humane level. When one contemplates relationships around a moral imperative, students say it best. What do students want when it comes to this concept? Hear their voices and listen to their words.

Students say the best teachers:

Know
us
personally.

1

All human beings have the desire for someone who cares about them enough to look beyond the outside and see what matters most. The desire for adults within the school who know students as individuals is paramount as one listens to what students say. Every person has the desire to feel special and appreciated. Richard Feynman captures the essence of this idea:

> *You can know the name of a bird in all the languages of the world, but when you're finished, you know absolutely nothing about the bird....So let's look at the bird and see what it's doing ...that's what counts. I learned very early the difference between knowing the name of something and knowing something.*

Often in schools, there is not a distinction between knowing the name of the students and knowing who students are as individuals. Schools must place more priority on learning about who students are, what they care about and what they do. As one student shared, "We want teachers not to judge us before they know us."

Students can express with much emotion and eloquence the impersonal nature of many schools. Consider the words of Sean Kopeny, a student who recounted the following in the book, *Welcome to Our World: Realities of High School Students*:

> The respect, or lack of it, that a student is shown in high school can greatly shape his or her future perceptions. In my high school, you were assigned an ID number and it was more important than your name; you get the feeling that you are little more than a number on an assembly line. Because the school is mass-producing students, it seems somewhat unimportant if they lose a couple of the many along the way" (Gilbert & Robins, 1998, p. 25).

This sense of disillusionment should haunt educators and schools. If students perceive that adults within the school are impervious to who they are as individuals or even if they believe the adults in the school are not troubled when we "lose" students, we have some soul-searching to do in our schools.

What are YOU or YOUR SCHOOL doing to learn who your students are?

Students say the best teachers:

Let us know who they are as individuals or people.

2

Relationships are dependent on two individuals having a common focus and understanding. Students not only want teachers to know them, they also want to know about the person who is instructing them. Before proceeding, it is incumbent to offer a disclaimer: we are not advocating the practice of students perceiving teachers as their best friends. When screening applicants for employment one of the responses often shared is, "I want students to know I'm their friend." We believe adults at school are there to be the child's teacher and to support and encourage students on their academic journey, not there to be their friend.

There must be a clear distinction between the role of the adult and the role of the students. However, that does not negate the fact that students need to know about their teachers. Who is my teacher? When disclosing information, care must be taken not to include intimate details. Students do not need to know about your personal problems. They want to know about your hobbies, interests, and pets, about why you entered the field of education and about your family. They want to be able to see you as a person and glean how that is reflected in their lives.

Students love the incorporation of stories from the teacher not only in content, but also in learning about the teacher. They are trying to decide the degree to which they will risk developing a relationship with the teacher. The highest compliment from students is the ability to employ the word, *mentor*, to capture the essence of the relationship they are seeking. Harry Wong (2001), an educational author, asserts there are seven things students want to know on the first day of school. Two relate to the need to identify personally with the teacher: Who is this teacher as a person? Will the teacher treat me as a human being? Relationships are predicated on trust. One way to help establish trust is seeing the person behind the label of educator.

What are YOU or YOUR SCHOOL doing to let students know who you are as people?

Students say the best teachers:

Smile at us.

3

A smile seems like such a simple gesture but the message it connotes to students is powerful. One would think that teachers would be cognizant of their body language and what it conveys to students. For students to list this as one of the things effective teachers do was surprising. As one begins to analyze why a smile is so important to students, it is directly related to students' perceptions around the question, "Does my teacher like me?" Although students never directly pose this question to teachers, never doubt it exists. Students answer it on the basis of their interaction with the teacher. As one high school student reflected, "I love to see my teacher smile. It makes me feel welcome and part of the class. It encourages me and I don't feel like I'm hated or my teacher is mad at me when I walk into class."

Every new teacher can recount hearing advice on classroom management about not smiling until Christmas. It is our belief one can have clear expectations and good classroom management while smiling at students. What's the first impression when someone walks into your school? What do you think your first impression might be to students based on your body language? More messages are conveyed by one's body language than by the words used when communicating. In fact, in face-to-face communication only seven percent (7%) of the message is based on the words used. Tone accounts for thirty-eight percent (38%) while fifty-five percent (55%) of communication is attributed to body language (Petersen & Karschnik, 2008, p. 1). Smiles are one of the most important aspects of body language, at least from a student perspective. It is evident students perceive classrooms with smiles as classrooms where someone wants them to be there and where someone will help them be successful. Students feel they have an ally, not an adversary when adults in school smile.

How often do YOU or others at YOUR SCHOOL smile at students?

Students say the best teachers:

Remember our names and use them.

4

It has been said that the sweetest sound to a person is the sound of his or her own name. The beginning of any relationship starts with an introduction and the exchange of names. It is difficult to conceive that classrooms might exist where educators do not take the time to learn the names of their students. Failure to learn and use students' names depersonalizes the learning process and negatively impacts the probability students will achieve at an optimum level. The least students can expect from their school experience is that the adults care enough about them to learn and use their names in class. It is an unforgivable act in the classroom for teachers not to know and use the names of their students.

Students report they like it when teachers see and treat them as individuals. One of the things that distinguish each of us from others is our name. It is the first step in learning who students are as individuals and recognizing their importance. Rapport cannot be established successfully without the use of students' names during interactions. Names are intertwined with identity and students use this as one of the yardsticks to measure their first impression of teachers. They want educators who care enough to know who they are. Every person has an unexpressed desire to be important to others and nothing is as important as when one is recognized in a positive and authentic manner using his or her name.

"What do you dislike about your school?" When students responded to this question, one high school student shared, "Many of our names aren't pronounced correctly. I am worried about graduation and that they won't pronounce our names right." School staff must take extra precautions to ensure they take the time to learn to pronounce difficult or unique names, conveying to students we appreciate not only the unique or beautiful nature of their name, but also the person who owns it.

How often do YOU or others at YOUR SCHOOL use the names of your students during interactions?

Students say the best teachers:

Speak to us.
They say hello
and good-bye.

5

The simplicity of the idea is not matched by the frequency of its occurrence in schools. While it may be proper etiquette or an expected social grace, evidently it is not a common practice. Speaking to students, saying hello or good-bye suggests the adults in the schools are *in the moment* with students. Every person likes to be spoken to and acknowledged. The best part of some students' day is while they are at school. Genuine interactions between teachers and students can foster a sense of belonging. During school or outside of school, students indicate their excitement when their teachers speak to them.

We had the opportunity to be in a high school setting for a period of time and happened to observe as students changed classes. Our observations left images in our minds that schools can be lonely and isolating places for some. It is disturbing to watch students walk down hallways with their heads down, avoiding eye contact with anyone. It is even more disturbing to see how many students this describes. No one spoke to these students and they did not interact with anyone. Do we notice the students in our schools? Are we so familiar with the landscape we fail to see what we don't want to see? Students have relatively low expectations when it comes to interactions with the adults at school. When students voice the one thing that was special about my teacher and it happens to be, "He speaks to me every day when I enter the classroom," the obvious realization is this is probably not occurring in many classrooms.

What would happen if we looked at our schools and our students with fresh eyes? What might we see or notice? What would happen if teachers committed to speaking to every student, especially those students who appear isolated? What would happen if, at the very least, teachers looked at these students, smiled, and said, "Hello, how are you today?" Or "Hello. I'm glad you're here today!" Take the time to notice and speak to your students.

How often do YOU or others at YOUR SCHOOL speak to your students?

Students say the best teachers:

Argue (banter, tease, joke) with us in a fun way in informal situations.

6

Students enjoy interacting with the adults in their schools. Everyone enjoys humor. Students report they like it when their teachers joke or banter with them in informal situations which may occur before or after class, in the hallways, in the lunchroom, or at different school functions. Teachers must do what is in their comfort zone. Some are good at telling stories, others at sharing appropriate jokes, while some might revert to quotes or cartoons. Students enjoy teachers stepping into their world for a minute or two and then stepping back out. They report enjoying teachers who "argue with them" about which ball team or soft drink is best, or teachers challenging students about being better at making baskets or turning cartwheels. This verbal and nonverbal playfulness is one way of inviting humor to be a frequent visitor in the classroom.

According to Performance Learning Systems (2002), humor in the classroom can yield positive results, especially for males. These include increasing student involvement, attention, and motivation, "enhancing group cohesion, and defusing tense situations" (p. 1). Humor can take many different forms. The key is using humor and verbal playfulness in a way that aligns with one's personality while creating an accepting and positive classroom environment.

One must share a cautionary tale related to humor in schools. Adults must be careful this bantering does not evolve into the use of sarcasm. Students despise sarcasm and interpret it as demeaning. Schools should not be characterized as places where sarcasm resides. A second aspect of the cautionary tale is that students are able to distinguish between appropriate and inappropriate use of humor. Effective teachers not only have a good sense of humor, but they are also able to get down to business and are in control of their classrooms.

How do YOU or others at YOUR SCHOOL interact with your students in fun ways?

Students say the best teachers:

Visit us at our homes before school starts.

7

We are cognizant that the idea of doing **home visits** frightens many educators and there are multiple reasons professionals share their **aversion** to this idea. However, students appreciate it when teachers take the time to visit them at **their homes**. Home visits make students feel special and provides the opportunity to not only **communicate** face –to-face, but also to communicate in an environment where the student **is comfortable**. Home visits convey to students you care about them and their world. **Students** maintain that teachers who "want to learn about us" are usually very effective teachers in **the classroom**.

Home visits not only make a difference for **students**, they leave a lasting impression in the lives of teachers. The following story from **Evelyn Bess** captures this.

Kathy Compton and I were on a home visit to see one of her new students. It was one of the most rewarding visits I have ever made.

You see – Caleb, age 4, lost his father to a heart attack this past June. His father was only 38 years old. Caleb's parents built the indoor dirt bike racing facility off the Double A highway.

Upon our arrival, we were given a tour of Caleb's home including meeting his pet cats (with baby kittens) and his two dogs. His mother shared the heartache their family had endured this summer while we watched Caleb play Spongebob on his Playstation. Her story warmed our hearts and touches our souls.

Mrs. Earlywine invited us to see "The Monster", the racing facility. They treated us to a fun ride as you can tell by the pictures. As we entered the building, Caleb turned and looked up with a twinkle in his eyes and asked, "Can you get your shoes a <u>little</u> dirty?"

"Sure!" we replied. We journeyed through the concession stands, up and down the bleachers and even onto the dirt track! It was great fun and quite an adventure for these two kindergarten teachers!

Afterwards, we loaded back up for our return to Caleb's house. Our final treat was to watch Caleb and his mother jumping together on the trampoline. His mother said that Caleb's father used to jump on the trampoline each night with him. I am glad his mother is continuing the tradition. I feel fortunate to witness and to see the joy of their smiles as they continue their lives – just mother and son.

As we were leaving, we were promised tickets ...to see Caleb compete in the 3-5 year olds quad-runner division in late October. Mrs. Compton and I can't wait to go!

The value of home visits is so much more than making connections. The visits ignite compassion, humility, and an understanding of ourselves, our students and their families.

Had to share...I am still on "Cloud Nine" after this visit! Have a great day!

How do YOU or others at YOUR SCHOOL get to know students and their parents??

Students say the best teachers:

Check on us when we are sick or even when we have sickness in our family.

8

Life has a way of rendering each of us vulnerable at certain times in our lives and no one is immune. Students need to know someone cares when illness or accidents occur. According to the American Youth Policy Forum in a publication entitled, *Some Things Make a Difference,* "Effective youth initiatives connect young people with adults who care about them, who serve as role models for them, who advise, mentor, chide, sympathize, encourage, and praise" (James, 1997, p. vi). If students or members of their family are ill, the adults at school can sympathize and encourage students.

There are a number of practices that convey to students you care about them when they or someone in their family is ill. Teachers in Mason County call home to talk to students if they miss two or three consecutive days. Some teachers call daily. They visit the hospitals, check on students at home, and send cards to let students know they are being thought about and missed. Some teachers even deliver homework and missed assignments to the students to get them back on track if students are well enough. One teacher calls home to students who are absent and the whole class shares in unison as the teacher holds the phone out to the class, "We miss you!"

Students are adept at learning lessons from our actions often more so than any outcome associated with direct instruction. Acts of compassion and empathy are never wasted.

> *Anthony, a middle school student, finds his way to the office twice a day. The front office staff expects his visit because he calls home to check on his mom who has a brain tumor. Once he hears her voice and enters into a brief conversation, he places the receiver on the phone, is given a reassuring smile and a pat on the shoulder with a follow-up inquiry about how things are going. He then returns to class.*

In most schools, would anyone even know about Anthony's situation? Is Anthony more focused on learning as a result of these actions? Nurturing hearts are often a prerequisite for nurturing minds.

How do YOU or others at YOUR SCHOOL show you care when students or members of their families are ill?

Students say the best teachers:

Remind us about school events and activities. They encourage us to participate.

9

Students want to feel connected to their school. One of the best avenues for this sense of connection is through student involvement in clubs and extracurricular activities. While many students do not need any prodding or hints about belonging to a club, team, or participating in a school function, there are those students who lack confidence and do not see themselves as a part of the school. They feel they are unable to contribute and fear others will see the flaws they see in themselves in lieu of the contributions each could make. By knowing the interests and gifts of each of the students, teachers can steer students in the right direction. In fact, some schools have a system established where teachers contact a sponsor or coach about a student and that person contacts the student, talks to them about their interests, and then extends an invitation for the student to become involved.

At our middle school, the eighth grade dance is a much-anticipated event at the end of the school year. Every year, some students did not attend the dance. However, after the home visit and making connections efforts at the school, school personnel started asking questions about why some students weren't planning on attending the dance. Often times, students would share they could not afford the dress or identify some other obstacle preventing them from participating. Teachers took it upon themselves to help make sure these obstacles were removed, often at their own expense. This was done quietly and without any fanfare or desire for recognition. These teachers created powerful memories for many middle school students, memories of belonging and not being excluded. We no longer assume students don't want to do things. Our teachers inquire and talk with students and silently often make the impossible, possible.

How do YOU or others at YOUR SCHOOL encourage student involvement in school activities?

Students say the best teachers:

Come see us perform in activities beyond the school day.

10

Our view of students is often limited to who we see in the classroom. The ability to see a different side to students, to see them excel or participate in activities in the school and community is one that should be pursued, when possible. Robert Haden, a student lamented, "To me, it seems that teachers never stop to think what a teen does outside the classroom…When teachers relate to students and make tiny inquiries, students feel more comfortable with the situation" (Gilbert & Robins, 1998, p. 35). Beyond making inquiries, the value of teachers taking time to watch a student in a play, a musical performance, a sporting event, or in an academic event should not be underestimated. It has an even greater impact when the teacher comments about the event when the student returns to school. Students do not want to disappoint adults when there is a reciprocal relationship based on caring. Frank, a student in a discussion group shared, "I would like my teacher not to really know me as a student, but as a person. I would like for the teachers to go to my game."

One of the most basic principles in customer service is thinking about an issue from the customer perspective. Lee Cockerell in the book, *Creating Magic* shares that one of Disney's four expectations is making the customer feel special (Cockerell, 2008, p. 53). A school administrator shared a story about one of the teachers at his school who attended the baseball game of one of her high school students. The teacher waved to the student and made sure he saw her. Throughout the game, the teacher cheered for this young man. This young man was overheard sharing with his teammates that the teacher was there for him, she was cheering for him! Her attendance at this event meant more to him than anyone will ever know. This is the first time an adult had ever attended one of his games to support him. His parents never saw him play the first game. Imagine how that young man felt about this teacher.

How often do YOU or others at YOUR SCHOOL attend events in the lives of your students?

Students say the best teachers:

Establish rules for everyone, including themselves.

11

Students need and want boundaries. It is a misnomer to believe that students do not want structure in the classroom. Rules are perceived by students to be expectations for appropriate behavior in the classroom. However, the kicker, as some students put it, is that rules must apply to everyone - without exception. One of the characteristics students assign to effective teachers is that they are "in control" in the classroom. Generally, control is equated with good classroom management and the belief that everyone in the class adheres to the same set of rules.

Students report it is important for teachers to mirror those rules and expectations in the classroom. For example, if the student cannot use a cell phone during class, the teacher should not use a cell phone during instructional time. This mutual agreement and adherence to how a classroom operates conveys a set of principles that governs classroom interactions. Students are perceptive and quick to sense the double standard resulting from a "Do as I say" versus a "Do what I do" expectation. Consider the following scenario.

> *A teacher discusses an expectation that the classroom will be based on respect among students, as well as between the teacher and student. The next day, a student repeatedly ignores a teacher's request to refrain from talking. Each time, the teacher's voice escalates and eventually the teacher states in a loud, stern voice "Are you deaf or something? Shut up!"*

It is not unusual for one to become frustrated from being ignored. It is also obvious the student's behavior did not mirror respect for the teacher. However, when the teacher responds in a demeaning manner to the student, students realize that bond of trust has been broken. Students expect, and rightfully so, the adults in schools should have high standards related to their own behavior and professionalism. Rules and expectations are important elements in creating a productive learning environment. Educators must be cognizant students perceive rules as a two way street with the unspoken etched into the minds of students.

How do YOU or others at YOUR SCHOOL ensure equitable and respectful adherence to rules for all students and for all staff?

Students say the best teachers:

Show no favoritism or perception of favoritism.

12

Students often perceive that some of their classmates receive a free pass and that decisions are made based on who one is. Favoritism is one of those emotional barometers students frequently check and are keenly alert to in the classroom. Students are quick to share one of the things they dislike the most is students having different privileges. Teachers must monitor their interactions and their words to ensure they are not consciously or subconsciously creating a favored student status in the classroom.

Athletes and academically talented students are two subgroups other students believe receive preferential treatment in classrooms. The belief that teachers embrace certain populations of students more than others often has its roots in how the school assigns students to classes. Favoritism can rear its ugly head when it comes to access to certain classes in schools. Futrell and Gomez (2008), researchers and educators, note practices such as ability grouping and tracking create a "poverty of learning" and suggests "students are well aware of the teaching and learning disparities that exist" in classrooms (p. 76). If we track students and constantly convey through actions that the school does not recognize every student has something to offer or contribute, students see through the hypocrisy. J.T. Gribbon describes his frustration with this practice:

> What I would like to know is why do you leave us in lower-level classes and learning disability classes and leave us out of a lot of your activities? It's kind of like saying we're not human, so we can't work with other students. Yes, it sounds cold as ice, but that's the way you make us feel. (Gilbert & Robins, 1998, p. 32).

I am unaware of any mission statement in schools that seeks to exclude students or make them feel like they're not human. It is incumbent on us to examine our words and our practices when it comes to how students perceive what is occurring in schools and in their classrooms.

How do YOU or others at YOUR SCHOOL ensure that favoritism doesn't exist in your classroom or school?

Students say the best teachers:

Are consistent.

13

The concept of consistency applies to various dimensions of the school experience. No one likes to be involved in a guessing game from day to day about what awaits them at school. Students become frustrated when they must constantly adjust to the mood of the adults in the building, determine what is acceptable or unacceptable in the classroom, or try to hit a moving target on what they need to do or learn. A productive learning environment is one where positive learning dispositions exist on a daily basis.

Students at the high school level can recount experiences in which they are allowed to do something one day and the next day they may receive a write-up for the same thing. Is it possible that students on the same team at a middle school can change classes and there are inconsistent rules and expectations from teacher to teacher? The result of either of these situations is the student has to try to "guess" what's appropriate from day to day. Students have very definite ideas about the inconsistency they experience:

- I find it extremely annoying when I go into a classroom never knowing what to expect. It is very stressful when the teacher is constantly changing his/her lesson plans and procedures.
- It makes me feel very confused and I lose respect for a teacher and I quit trying to catch up on the new expectation.
- I wish they would just set one standard, not too low, and stick with it. It gives the students hope.
- It makes me feel frustrated when a teacher changes the way he/she runs the class. It takes time away from what needs to be done. It doesn't help if they can't control the class from the beginning. If we students know you can't take charge, then we will not respect you as our teacher.
- It makes me feel challenged at times, but then when the expectations are lowered and the class is too easy, I dislike it.

It's the students who must "read" the situation and then readjust their behavior and actions based on their analysis of the situation. As one student noted, "It throws us off." Therefore, students are constantly adjusting to change and identifying inconsistencies in expectations.

How do YOU or others at YOUR SCHOOL ensure there is consistency in your interactions and practices?

Students say the best teachers:

Cook (or do something special) for us.

14

Students are able to recall with vivid detail not only memorable experiences in schools, but negative ones which made them feel humiliated or embarrassed. However, when discussing what the best teachers did, students reminisced with excitement and enthusiasm about school experiences which made them feel special. They could take you back in time and offer you a descriptive depiction. Students were able to elaborate on experiences such as:

- I love it when my teachers try to make things for us even if it's something small. In eighth grade my teacher…gave us all cards that had our names in Japanese for Christmas. I still have mine today.
- Makes me feel like they care more than just having a job like when our homeroom teacher bought pizza for us out of her pocket.
- When students in my class reached their goal, the teacher had a "lock-in" at school on Friday night and planned lots of fun activities.

Students enjoy it when a teacher who has a special skill or talent finds a way to share it with his or her class. One skill students often attribute to some of their teachers is cooking. We are not advocating everyone cook for students. We are suggesting, based on student interviews, students are enamored with educators who find a way to include students in their interests or do something for students beyond the act of teaching. Students in Cheri Johnson's homeroom at the high school express their excitement when Mrs. Johnson bakes monkey bread and brings it to school. They know she is taking her own personal time to do something for them and this is something they can enjoy and experience as a class. One student from Mrs. Johnson's homeroom shared the only reason she had not dropped out of school was she knew her teacher really cared about her. She became pregnant between her junior and senior years. Mrs. Johnson had a baby shower for her and encouraged her to stay in school. Cooking for students and hosting baby showers are not included in any teacher's job description, but they are important to students. They are cognizant their teacher cares about students enough to do the little extras.

How do YOU or others at YOUR SCHOOL make students feel special?

Students say the best teachers:

Know we are always watching. We observe their behavior before, during, and after school.

15

Teachers are always on stage. Do you treat students one way in class and then hide or ignore them if you see them at the grocery? Do you put them down in front of other students or other teachers? Do you make promises and then offer excuses about why you didn't follow through? Do you acknowledge students when you see them outside the classroom? As adults and role models, teachers are instrumental in the lives of students. Students observe you and are keenly aware of any discrepancy between what you say and what you do. Malcolm, a high school student, describes this discrepancy as a teacher who just puts in time as opposed to those teachers who do everything they can to help you.

Students want teachers who walk the talk, who are genuine in their interactions, who view teaching not as a job, but as a difference-maker for students. Students are looking for adults whose temperaments are consistent, whose efforts direct their paths in a positive direction, and whose encouragement sustains them when they fail or experience self-doubt. When this is the case, the pay-off for both parties is great. Nel Noddings, a professor at Stanford University, conveys the type of pay-off that is possible. She writes, "At a time when the traditional structures of caring have deteriorated, schools must become places where teachers and students live together, talk with each other, take delight in each other's company…it is obvious that children will work harder and do things – even odd things like adding fractions – for people they trust" (Noddings, 1988, p. 32). Students observe you in various settings because they want to know they can trust you.

What would students share about YOU or others at YOUR SCHOOL based on their observations throughout the day?

The Lesson for Educators

"Be true to your work, your word, and your friend." Educators would be wise to adapt the words of Henry David Thoreau and professionally abide by the words: *Be true to our work, our word, and our students.* Relationships around a moral imperative is the foundational element in forging relationships within schools. When one consults professional literature, there is a plethora of evidence to support the inclusion of efforts geared toward building and sustaining relationships as schools work to create productive environments for learning. We must commit to building and sustaining relationships even though there may be some who shy away from this premise. As educators, we have a moral imperative to do so.

How can we recapture the attention, imagination, motivation, and commitment of students to the learning process? Not only do educational researchers provide direction to this inquiry, but students can succinctly and unequivocally articulate how schools and educators can achieve this outcome. The vocabulary may differ from the research voice and from the student voice, but the ideas are analogous. They are interwoven and interrelated to the degree it is often difficult to differentiate who is doing the speaking. Although students articulated descriptions in more simplistic and discrete categories, the evolution of ideas and their importance from each perspective offers rich discussion opportunities for teachers and schools.

The following graphic organizer allows one to make his or her own comparisons by presenting an overview of all the concepts from the research, as well as the student voice. It offers a snapshot of ideas from both perspectives. As you compare the ideas in the first column of the organizer to what students said, it is evident the two are strikingly similar. Perhaps, educators should strive to also be true to our students by listening to their voices because it is the right thing to do for all involved.

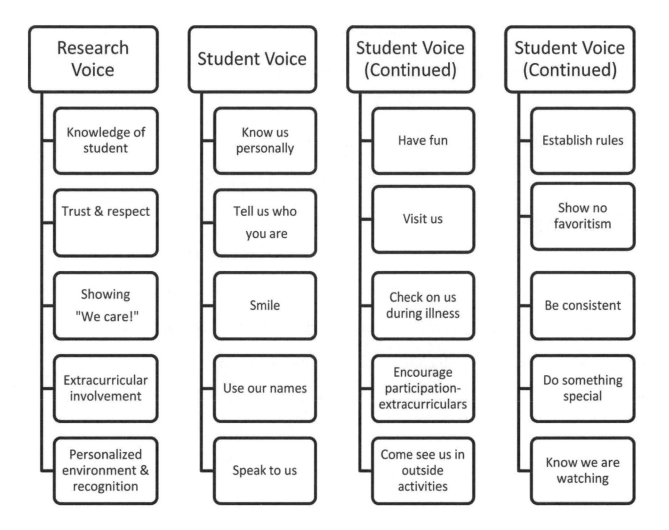

Research Voice	Student Voice	Student Voice (Continued)	Student Voice (Continued)
Knowledge of student	Know us personally	Have fun	Establish rules
Trust & respect	Tell us who you are	Visit us	Show no favoritism
Showing "We care!"	Smile	Check on us during illness	Be consistent
Extracurricular involvement	Use our names	Encourage participation-extracurriculars	Do something special
Personalized environment & recognition	Speak to us	Come see us in outside activities	Know we are watching

Comparisons suggest the ideas presented within each category parallel the other conceptually, with the exception of students recounting specific attributes of a personalized learning environment that includes recognition. One should not assume that personalization and recognition are not significant to students. Even though they shared ways accomplishments were celebrated by teachers, students gravitated more toward describing the behavior of the teacher as opposed to the importance of a personalized environment and recognition. Reviewing some of the questions posed under the category of personalized learning and recognition at the beginning of this chapter, it is evident the ideas are encompassed in other descriptions shared by students.

When engaging students in dialogue about perspectives related to their education and what happens in schools and classrooms, it is apparent that relationships around a moral imperative, or because it is the right thing to do, dominate the discussion. Educators must be willing to read between the lines about the critical nature of the interactions occurring in schools. It is so important to students they distinguish between the subtleties of our words and actions, and internalize each at such a level it is often difficult to unravel the intricate way students create a verbal sculpture depicting their school life. If relationships are not initially pursued with intentionality and authenticity, schools have not only missed a golden opportunity to change the cultures of their schools, they may even negate the impact of other school reform or improvement efforts. To put it bluntly, students will turn off to school and become more chronically disengaged because no one takes the time to care, hold them accountable, and help them be successful.

As one reviews the list of comments from students, there is nothing earth-shattering in terms of expectations. They appear to be attainable, require few resources, and should just be a part of how we interact with others. What *is* earth-shattering is students' perceptions these behaviors are not part of their existing school culture. The take-away message from what students say is that as teachers and school personnel, we are always on stage and as Marzano (2007) purposefully uses in his phrase consisting of a double negative, students are never not watching.

The Lesson for Educators

We need to not only make a personal connection with our students,
but also an emotional one!

Trip Down Memory Lane Reflection

All of us have a history, a personal story to be told. If you were to reflect on your history as a learner, what lessons might inform your interactions with students in the classroom? The following questions were developed around the student voice within this chapter as a guide in recalling your own story.

1. As a learner, how did knowing "why you needed to do things" enable you to be more successful?

2. Did a teacher's love of his/her subject matter ever inspire you to give more of yourself to a class? How did that teacher convey passion for the subject area and his/her enjoyment for teaching?

3. Did you ever get involved in an extracurricular activity because of a teacher or coach? What did he/she say or do that made you want to become involved in that activity?

4. Did you ever have a teacher who stopped and checked on you at home or attended one of your afterschool activities? How did that make you feel? Was your attitude, effort, or work different in this classroom than others?

5. Did you ever have a teacher who told you a little about who he/she was as a person or what his/her experience was like as a student? Did this strengthen your connection with the teacher?

6. Did you ever have a teacher who liked to argue with you or tease you in a fun way? How did that make you feel? Did this cause you to want to work harder?

Write down some phrases you might use to describe your story as a learner.

_____

_____

_____

How will your story influence your expectations and actions as a teacher?

_____

_____

_____

Professional Reflection

In my school:

Questions were listed at the end of each student voice description. After looking at these questions or reviewing the graphic organizer depicting the research and the student voice, think about what your school does well and what would be some areas identified for improvement. Identify two to three areas of strength for your school and place in the appropriate column. Identify two or three areas you would like for your school to consider investigating.

Areas of strength at my school:	Areas I wish my school would target:

In my classroom:

As you think about the ideas presented in this chapter, identify what was especially meaningful for you. What are two or three ideas you will make a commitment to doing in your class? Write these ideas in the space provided.

I commit to doing the following things in my school or classroom:

Chapter 3

Relationships Around Curriculum

Let us think of education as the means of developing our greatest abilities, because in each of us is a private hope and dream which, fulfilled, can be translated into benefit for everyone and greater strength of the nation.

-John F. Kennedy

Relationships Around Curriculum Research Voice

Martin Luther King, Jr. once shared, "You don't have to see the whole staircase, just take the first step." Although building relationships and making connections is a crucial initial step, getting to the top of the staircase where teachers take academic ownership of their students is often a steep climb. It's not the desire that is lacking, but the overwhelming challenge of taking all the parts and putting them together in ways that make significant differences to students. The complexity is not in the idea, it is in systematically putting the various components into place regarding curriculum, instruction, and assessment in a way that enables all students to be successful.

Educators can also think about relationships in the context of the curriculum. One of the most important aspects in lesson planning after determining objectives and assessments is entertaining the question, "How will I get students engaged in the content?" Research is replete with conclusions supporting the correlation between student achievement and student engagement. Getting students actively involved in the content *hooks* them to the lesson and creates a greater likelihood they will be successful understanding the content. Relationships as they apply to the curriculum, and based on the research voice focuses on the importance of various elements including: incorporating relevance, capitalizing on students' interests, accessing background knowledge, sharing learning goals, fostering interdisciplinary connections, and displaying student work.

Relationships Around

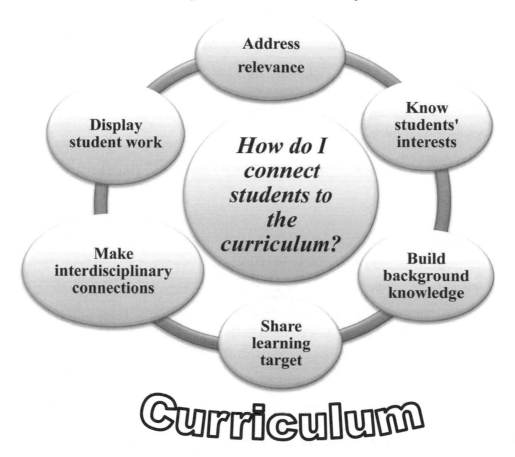

Curriculum

One of the best ways of getting students engaged in the curriculum is knowing the

students and then finding ways to connect them to what they will be learning. Those with

classroom experience are keenly aware one of the first questions posed by students is "Why do I

need to know this?" Students need to know why the content they are learning is important and

how it relates to "real life." This is referred to as *relevance* and as professionals we need to

ensure that relevance is systematically addressed and shared with students. An arduous task of

educators is designing learning experiences that are meaningful and purposeful to students.

Knowing how content can be applied in the world of work or in everyday life helps establish a sense of purpose. John Malouff (2008), an instructor at the University of New England School of Psychology in Australia, and some of his colleagues identified twelve methods for increasing student motivation. Making content relevant to student values and goals was identified as a category. They advocate:

> Teach topics in a way that has potential for immediate application and possible benefit to students, e.g. if the topic is self control strategies such as overeating, go beyond discussing the problem and encourage students to test self-control strategies such as goal setting and self-monitoring to regulate their own eating" (p. 3).

All too often, we assume students can connect the dots and indirectly establish the relevance for what they are learning. In the book, *Activating the Desire to Learn*, Bob Sullo shares a reflection of a high school student in the last chapter of the book. Matt, a high school senior, comments on relevance. He believes:

> Unskilled teachers do not adequately explain the usefulness of what is being taught. They take it for granted that students will understand the relevance of the lesson and will work hard. Unless students have an especially strong connection with the teacher, they will only do their best work when they fully understand why it is important.

Students know! Matt's analysis provides valuable insight. Unless students have a relationship with the teacher, the next method with the greatest likelihood for success is relevance. Students know the difference between effective and ineffective teachers. Matt continues his reflection noting:

> Effective teachers provide specific examples of how learning can be applied by students in a way that is relevant to them. Once students see the relevance of what they are asked to do, their natural; internal motivation leads them to do higher-quality academic work (Sullo, 2007, pp. 152-153).

Barr and Parrett (2007) convey that *relevance* is often rooted in knowing the student in his/her world. They advocate knowledge of the student, as well as the student's environment noting, "Another key to student's motivation to learn lies in a teacher's ability to see this connection to the content and find its relevance to a student's everyday life and world" (p.198).

Other educators concur and elaborate on the how relevance enhances motivation. Malouff and

his associates at the University of New England School of Psychology in Australia assert that

making content relevant to student values and goals impacts motivation. Recommendations

include:

   A. Teach topics in a way that has potential for immediate application and possible
       benefit to students.
   B. Before each class session, remind yourself why the material is meaningful and
       interesting.
   C. Relate subject matter to the specific interests of students.
   D. Relate subject matter to the everyday experiences of students.
   E. Ask students to give personal examples of applications of principles being studied.
   F. Give students choice about what they learn, e.g., what topics are covered in class and
       in assignments. (Malouff, et al, 2008, p. 3).

Other research organizations affirm and support the importance of these ideas for

improving student achievement. Insights by researchers Akey (2006) and Heller et al (2003) are

shared in an article entitled, "Using Positive Student Engagement to Increase Student

Achievement."

   Students learn more and retain more when they actively participate in the learning
   process and when they can relate to what is being taught…Drawing connections between
   information taught and real life – such as everyday life, social issues, and personal
   concerns of the age groups of students is highly effective in engaging students in the
   lesson (p. 2).

Drawing connections doesn't happen naturally. It is the difference between being the artist or

just buying a piece of artwork. When one contemplates relationships around curriculum,

relevance is the brush for painting on a blank canvas. Emptiness is replaced with colorful

strokes with each student being his own artist and finding meaning in the subject matter and

learning they are creating. Curricular experiences void of relevance results in students being merely consumers of curriculum and content with little regard for what they can create or how they will be able to use the content they are learning.

Relationships are instrumental in providing a vehicle for teachers to incorporate *students' interests* to the curriculum being studied. Robert Marzano (2007) postulates incorporating student interests promotes an atmosphere of concern and cooperation in the classroom. He also suggests "creating metaphors and creating analogies...are perfect vehicles for designing tasks around student interests" (p. 156). In a newsletter from the Center for Comprehensive School Reform and Improvement in 2007, research is cited highlighting the importance of capitalizing on students' interests asserting, "Inclusion of students' interests in the learning process increases student engagement in learning" (p. 2). Student interests can also serve as a bridge for building the relevance of a lesson. Knowledge of the students, their learning styles, and what motivates them enables teachers to seek opportunities to link the curriculum to students' interests. These can serve as the basis for multiple pathways to the curriculum. From the teacher making a recommendation about a book to the development of a product to demonstrate learning, knowledge of student interests allows teachers and students to capitalize on curricular connections.

The third factor one needs to consider when thinking about relationships around the curriculum is the *background knowledge* of students. What knowledge do students bring to the learning or the task? How can we activate and build on this academic knowledge? These are two of the guiding questions that shape curricular planning. Research suggests there is a strong correlation between background knowledge and student achievement. Educators must not only be concerned with purposefully addressing background knowledge during curricular decision-making, they must also be cognizant of the discrepancy that exists in students' background knowledge based on their experiences, as well as the discriminating variable of poverty. In the book, *Building Background Knowledge for Academic Achievement*, Robert Marzano (2004) notes " …given the relationship between academic background knowledge and academic achievement, one can make the case that it should be at the top of any list of interventions intended to enhance student achievement" (p. 4). In fact, Marzano continues by providing educators with a warning: "If not addressed by schools, academic background can create great advantages for some students and great disadvantages for others" (p.4). There are a variety of resources and techniques teachers can utilize for developing background knowledge. However, one must know the students and understand students come to an academic task and to content with varying levels of background knowledge. If the goal is to link students to the curriculum, accessing and building background knowledge plays a vital role in establishing that link.

When considering key attributes of the curriculum from the student perspective, an important aspect is clarity with regard to the *goal* of the lesson. As Marzano (2009) surmises, "The terms goals and objectives are often used interchangeably" in educational literature (p. 3). Another term associated with goals of a lesson is *learning targets*. Recommendations from contemporary resources suggest educators should start with clear learning goals and then develop these into student-friendly learning targets. Regardless of the term used, expectations should not be a secret. Telling students what you want them to learn enables them to progress along a continuum from their own understanding to concepts and ideas conveyed through the curriculum. A teacher must be clear about a learning target before it is communicated to students. When students know what they are suppose to be learning, student achievement increases from 16 to 41 percentile points (with an average of 21 percentile points) (Marzano, 2007, p.11). Professional resources are available to guide educators in the development and use of learning targets, including writing the targets in student-friendly terms. This personalizes the learning for students. When students are able to finish the statements beginning with *I can* or *I know*, they are clear about what should take away from the lesson. Stiggins (2008) asserts that learning targets empower students, putting them in charge of their own learning. Learners can reflect on their own understanding, as well as ask questions related to the target. Students would like for us to help them solve the mystery of day-to-day expectations regarding the curriculum by sharing learning targets with them.

Another way educators can address relationships around curriculum is to help students make connections among content by incorporating *interdisciplinary* lessons. Most students experience with content comes in isolated sound bites with little, if any consideration of how different content areas relate to one another. When teachers can collaboratively plan and integrate curricular ideas using a thematic or inquiry approach, the content makes more sense and students views learning more as an integrated process.

Finally, students desire to be part of a classroom characterized by an environment which conveys "I value your work and how you make sense of the content." One way to do this is to *display student work*. Displaying quality student work sends powerful messages to students related to curriculum. Think about how displaying student work might be interpreted by the students. Students may feel a greater sense of ownership of the classroom and their learning. They are aware that learning can be shared in a variety of ways. They have visual models and reminders about their learning. They may feel validated knowing the teacher wishes to showcase the work with others. During curricular planning, opportunities for sharing student learning and for showcasing curricular understandings should be sought. Displays are one form of recognition and everyone craves some level of positive recognition.

Students Speak: What Our Customers Say

Relationships serve as a point of departure as teachers map out curricular experiences for students. Students know when a classroom is "their" classroom. They also know when the teacher is the sole proprietor of the classroom. Academic knowledge and how to apply it in appropriate situations is a goal of schools. The burgeoning of content expected to be taught and to be mastered by students sometimes leads to covering the content, as opposed to learning the content. What gets taught in schools is critical. Understanding how students perceive the curriculum and what enables them to become "friends" with it, as opposed to ignoring it enables educators to be more deliberate in their planning efforts related to the curriculum. Students know when lessons are carefully crafted with them in mind because curricula designed around relationships answer many of the questions students have without them ever having to ask. What do students want when it comes to this concept? Hear their voices and listen to their words.

Students say the best teachers:

Tell us why.

16

At birth, children seem to have an insatiable curiosity about the world and how it works. How difficult is it to recall observing a parent with a small child who wonders why the sky is blue and the grass is green? Many adults tire of hearing why after why question from young children, but the fact remains that even as adults, we want to know why we are asked to engage in certain practices. Some research suggests that when a statement is followed by the word *because,* attention increases exponentially.

Students share the following advice, "Tell us why we need to do things. We respond better if you tell us why." In the same breath, students are quick to add, "Telling us we need to learn or do something because I say so or because it is in a textbook or curriculum guide is not the why we need answered." John Maxwell, who writes extensively on leadership, would share these students demonstrate an astuteness in this response. They are reacting as most adults do when someone uses a "because I said so" reply. Maxwell (2007) refers to this as the lowest level of leadership which he describes as people following because of position or rights – because they have to and are forced to feel they do not have a choice. It's an "I'm the boss" mentality. Regardless, everyone (adults and students) need to know why and respond more positively if the response is thoughtful and clearly stated.

We need to learn this because….; You need to do this because….; If you learn how to ____, you will be able to ____ – there's something about adding the word *because* to a statement or telling a person why that makes everyone listen and react more positively. Somehow the word because gets left out of discussions at school. We are quick to address what we need to do but seldom take the time to explain why. Students want to know why.

How do YOU or others at YOUR SCHOOL make sure that the WHY is explained to your students in all classrooms?

Students say the best teachers:

Tell us how we will use what we are learning in the real world.

17

Tell us how we will use what we learn is a close relative of telling us why we need to engage in certain behaviors or practices. However, the screams of students at every level are deafening when it comes to understanding the importance of this concept in curricular experiences. There are two nuances pointing a finger at current practices in school based on this response from students. First, students interpret school experiences as something distinct and very different from what one is required to do in the real world. Secondly, it is obvious from students' perspectives that discussions focused on how one can use information and how it applies to the real world is nonexistent in many classrooms. If one doubts these assumptions, just review some of the phrases used by educators to describe the artificiality that students have identified. When encountering educational resources, how often are terms such as authentic learning experiences and real-world application touted as being important elements when planning curricular opportunities for students?

Relevance is one of the key principles students continually refer to in their conversations about school experiences and in their delineation of effective teachers. If we polled students as they exited classrooms throughout the country and solicited a response to the question, How *might one apply or use the information you are studying?* What percentage of students could provide an acceptable response? Most would fear what students might say. However, it is apparent from listening to students they not only like knowing real life application, but they also respond favorably to classroom experiences where teachers are engaged in interdisciplinary studies where they can see the interconnectedness of the ideas they are learning.

How do YOU or others at YOUR SCHOOL address relevance of content?

Students say the best teachers:

Help us learn about our future and our role in making it better (e.g. "going green").

18

Students want to take an active role in their own futures. They want to make connections about the content they are learning with issues that will impact them in their future. They are cognizant the world is complex and is constantly changing. However, students want to make a difference and examine their roles as students and as future citizens within their communities. Curriculum needs to capitalize on these intrinsic elements whenever possible. Educators must look for opportunities to infuse ideas into the curriculum for discussion and action that relate to the future and how each person can make a difference. We must incorporate higher level thinking skills where we analyze situations, or where students problem solve how things could function differently, with an eye and an ear toward becoming more responsible citizens. We must incorporate curricular experiences where students understand all actions have a level of accountability with regard to the environment and the world we leave for future generations.

What opportunities exist in the curriculum and in extracurricular endeavors enabling schools to achieve this goal? Are students involved in service projects in the community? Are schools utilizing students and involving them in environmental or going green initiatives? Do we forego exchange of gifts in classrooms so we can do a drive for the food bank or adopt a name from an angel tree? Do we identify issues within our community and then form a plan of action to address a need? Students need to know they can and do make a difference with their input, collective action, and involvement. There are multiple social and environmental issues providing the springboard where students can experience that being a citizen requires active involvement, not blind acceptance.

***How do YOU or others at YOUR SCHOOL
incorporate roles students can play or projects they can do
enabling them to make a difference in their world
and the future of others?***

The Lesson for Educators

What gets taught in classrooms is extremely important. While students often feel they have no control over what gets taught, teachers express frustration about the extent of their decision-making efforts regarding curriculum. Curriculum is often articulated by standards and core content identified by national, state, or even professional organizations. While curricular concepts may be identified by others, teachers and students can exercise greater control over the context and how these concepts are presented. One of the avenues to accomplish this feat is to rethink approaches to curricular experiences using voices from research, as well as suggestions from the student voice. No one will debate the importance of rigor in the curriculum; however, when students discuss effective teachers, they hunger for experiences relating primarily to relevance with an appropriate level of challenge.

Comparisons between the research voice and the student voice demonstrate an almost sixth sense of students in knowing best practices. Students may not be the authors of curriculum standards or core learning recommendations; however, they are astute in their reflections conveying their need to understand the significance of content presented. One can observe how some of the practices identified from each of the categories, research voice, and student voice, mirror each other.

A second observation from comparison of the voices suggests that, although background experience and displaying work related to curriculum being studied were not alluded to by the students; these two areas offer opportunities for students to make connections to the curriculum. Assessing and building background knowledge offer points of departure for accessing the curriculum. Displaying student work are artifacts which demonstrate how students come to make sense of the content they are learning.

92

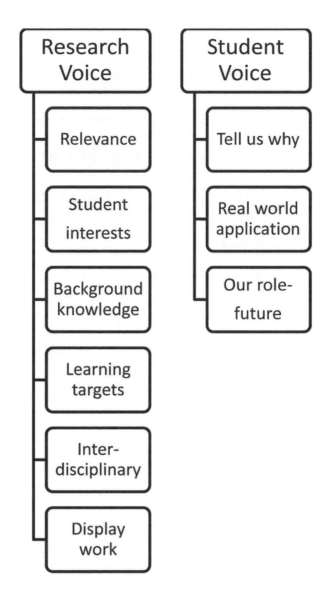

Consideration of the question, "What will I do to connect students to the curriculum?" necessitates educators complete the prerequisite course of forming relationships, and knowing the students. Relationships around curriculum build on that initial course. As Scott Gengler, principal of a Minnesota high school once commented, "Our curriculum is better because of our commitment to build positive connections with all students before anything else. We focus on building constructive relationships with students and providing educational experiences for them that they will treasure for years." (Ramsey, 2008, p. 148). By listening to the student voice,

those curricular experiences become more meaningful.

The Lesson for Educators

Students have an intrinsic need to make sense of what they are learning and
are more motivated if they are provided a context for their learning.
Relevance should be explicitly addressed in curricular experiences.

A Trip Down Memory Lane Reflection

*Continue to reflect on your history as a **learner** that you started in previous chapters. Use the following questions related to curricular experiences as a guide.*

1. Think about a lesson or unit that captured your attention and made you want to learn more. What was it about this lesson or unit that created this reaction?

2. Recall a time when your work was displayed. Why was it displayed and how did it make you feel?

3. Relevance is an important consideration in curricular planning. Recall an experience where the teacher emphasized relevance. How did you respond as a learner?

Record any ideas from your memories about curricular experiences that you could apply to your classroom.

_____
_____
_____
_____
_____
_____

Professional Reflection

In my school:

Questions were listed at the end of each student voice description. After looking at these questions or reviewing the graphic organizer depicting the research and the student voice, think about what your school does well and what would be some areas identified for improvement. Identify one or two areas of strength for your school and place in the appropriate column. Identify one or two areas you would like for your school to investigate to make a difference in your school.

Areas of strength at my school:	Areas I wish my school would target:

In my classroom:

As you think about the ideas presented in this chapter, identify what was especially meaningful for you. What are one or two ideas you would make a commitment to doing in your class? Write these ideas in the space below.

I commit to doing the following things in my school or classroom:

Chapter 4

Relationships Around Instruction

Good teaching is more a giving of right questions than a giving of right answers.

-Josef Albers

Once children learn how to learn, nothing is going to narrow their mind. The essence of teaching is to make learning contagious, to have one idea spark another.

-Marva Collins

Relationships Around Instruction Research Voice

From thinking about what we teach in relation to who we teach, the next connection to be made is framing the concept of relationships around instruction. Who we teach and how we teach it are inextricably linked; yet, these two concepts may not result in deliberate planning that plays on the interaction of those ideas. The guiding question for educators who are reflecting about relationships around instruction is, "How can I promote student learning?" Contemplation of this question is especially important with findings from various research studies such as the one cited in the book, *Results Now: How We Can Achieve Unprecedented Improvements in Teaching and Learning.* Based on 1,500 classroom observations, the following trends were documented:

- In 85% of the classrooms observed, "Fewer than one-half of the students were paying attention";
- In 52% of the classrooms observed, "Students were using worksheets"; and
- In 3% of the classrooms observed, "There was evidence of higher-order thinking" (Schmoker, 2006, p. 18).

One would have to question the amount of learning occurring, especially if the classrooms observed are representative of classrooms everywhere. Envision these classrooms where students are relegated to passive roles as learners. These trends are an indictment of the instructional strategies being utilized. There are a myriad of resources which can be consulted to address the question of practices supporting student learning. However, when one imagines the identification of instructional practices with relationships in mind, certain concepts emerge. The following organizer provides one with an overview of instructional practices leveraging the power of relationships.

Relationships Around

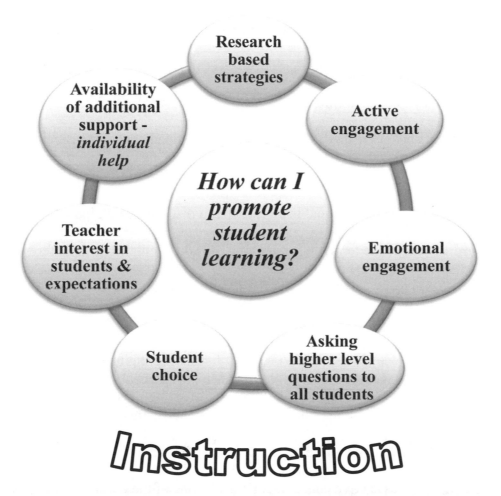

Research based strategies

Active engagement

Availability of additional support - *individual help*

How can I promote student learning?

Emotional engagement

Teacher interest in students & expectations

Student choice

Asking higher level questions to all students

Instruction

As one peruses the different focal points identified related to instruction, those focal points can be grouped into two categories: one has to do with instructional practices the teacher utilizes; the other focuses on words and actions of the teacher as he/she interacts with students.

Initially, *research based* instructional practices should serve as the roadmap to a learning destination. However, one must realize that incorporation of research based strategies requires decision-makers to identify and prioritize those strategies, seeking ones which are high leverage. One must also note that training in a research based strategy requires time, persistence, and opportunity for planning, integration, implementation, and reflection before it can become part of a repertoire of strategies for teachers. This must be done systematically using a common vocabulary and a common process among faculty with an emphasis on how the strategy impacts student learning. Contemporary educators should consult the knowledge base which currently exists when matching strategies to instructional needs.

Active engagement strikes at the heart of the learning process. Barr and Parrett (2007) encourage educators to "make learning active, hands-on, and when possible, enjoyable" suggesting all students benefit, especially underachieving students when teachers plan lessons where students have the "opportunity to actively learn" (p. 199). While it is a goal of the instructional process, achieving the goal is more difficult than often anticipated. One of the reasons for this difficulty is the term, engagement, means different things to different people. Robert Marzano (2007) offers educators with the spectrum of conceptualizations and then uses a synthesis of ideas compiled by Reeve who states:

> Engagement includes on-task behavior, but it further highlights the central role of students' emotions, cognition, and voice…When engagement is characterized by the full range of on-task behavior, positive emotion, invested cognition, and personal voice, it functions as the engine for learning and development. (p. 99).

Whether one perceives engagement as participation, as hands-on learning, or one making sense of learning in their own way, active engagement must be one of the cornerstones of lesson design. Maybe educators should follow the advice of Alfie Kohn, author of the book, *Beyond Discipline* who suggests we ask ourselves the question, "When students are 'off-task,' our first question should be, What's the task?" (Kohn, 2006, p. 19).

Emotional engagement is one of the best ways of ensuring active learning by students. Emotion can play such a critical role in learning, yet it is one that is often neglected during instructional planning. David Kobrin (2004) in the book, *In There With the Kids* discusses a scenario involving a teacher who planned a lesson for students with the premise, "….any learning that goes beyond the academic to include the emotional will be moving…" (p. 192).

Issues, simulations, mystery situations, debates, and multiple perspectives are a few common entry activities geared not only toward an inquiry approach to learning, but also geared toward getting students immersed into the content emotionally. Eric Jensen (2005) shares emotion is one of the best avenues for engaging the brain in learning. He utilizes the term "engineered controversy" to suggest that learning is enhanced when educators judiciously use situations to pull learners into the content. However, one should navigate these emotional territories carefully. Emotional connections to the lesson should never embarrass students or get them so emotionally aroused, they are unable to view an issue from other points of view.

Questioning is one of the best techniques in a teacher's toolbox, even if it is not used as effectively as it could be. The key is asking *higher level questions for all students*. Many research studies lament the type and frequency of questioning characterized as low level questioning because it requires little thought process on the part of students. Assumptions are often made about students, especially students from poverty. According to Fisher and Frey (2007) who summarize some of the findings related to instruction and students from poverty:

> …teachers talk more and students talk less…In addition, there is an increased focus on basic skills in these classrooms and less attention to critical and creative thinking. Teachers of struggling student groups or tracks usually offer students 'less exciting, less emphasis on meaning and conceptualization, and more rote drill and practice activities' than teachers of high performing or heterogeneous groups and classes. (p. 21).

One of the most important outcomes in education is for students to think critically and creatively about ideas. If students are not exposed to anything other than basic comprehension questions, it is unlikely they will be able to achieve this outcome.

Choice is a powerful motivator. Every person not only likes choice, but has come to expect it in today's society. Somehow, the concept of choice has not found its way to the classroom, nor in instructional planning. Relationships around instruction must include a healthy

dose of *student choice*. Student choice can be achieved in multiple ways including "having some

ownership over the routines and protocols of the classroom" (Jackson, 2009, p. 43). The most

common conceptualization of choice in the classroom involves assignments. Teachers can

"build in opportunities for students to have some influence or control in what goes on in the

classroom. Give students choices about how to complete assignments that best fit their own

learning styles, interests, and needs" (Jackson, 2009, p. 47). This is not to suggest students must

have choice on every assignment. However, choice should not be a visitor to classroom

instruction – something we see only once or twice. When that occurs, we negate the influence of

a powerful motivator.

Every student in every classroom secretly longs to become part of a classroom where the

teacher conveys in words and actions that, "I believe in you and I believe you can succeed!"

Fear of failure is one of the leading reasons people often fail to try. *Teacher interest in students*

goes beyond knowing the student and extends to having *high expectations* for each student. Barr

and Parrett (2008), noted educators and authors, share the following:

> Public education effectively teaches the top 20 or 30 percent of enrolled students. The
> challenge comes when high academic performance is expected of the other 70 percent. It
> is this group of students, many of whom are apathetic, bored, unmotivated, and often
> disruptive that represents the greatest challenge for teachers and schools. The good news
> is that a growing number of schools nationwide have become increasingly successful
> with this demanding, often neglected majority. Even better, researchers have begun to
> document specific instructional approaches that can dramatically improve academic
> achievement. Students will live 'up to' or 'down to' our expectations (p.193).

Students living up to expectations can be achieved by employing effective strategies and

having a variety of support mechanisms in place. Providing students with *additional support*

and individual help communicates to students the school wants them to succeed. Unfortunately,

in this place called school, the motto is often "one and done". Students are presented with content and are expected to demonstrate mastery based on this initial encounter. Schools and teachers need to reflect on the question posed by DuFour and his colleagues, "What happens when students don't learn?" This is an area of growth for all schools. If the goal of school is learning by students, then conversations in schools need to delineate ways teachers can assist students who need additional help.

Promoting excellence in schools is achieved not only through accessing students to curriculum, but also through purposeful selection of instructional strategies where students interact and experience the curriculum. The pursuit of excellence is directly tied to teacher expectations and teacher behaviors. Effective educators keep students at the heart of their efforts when designing learning experiences for their students.

Students Speak: What Our Customers Say

The research voice provides guidance for educators about instructional paths that should be pursued to enhance learning opportunities for students. While there are many professional resources that delineate an array of instructional practices that support learning, and these resources offer explicit guidance regarding implementation, the instructional practices selected for this chapter present common threads among various researchers. Relationships around instruction compels educators to look for strategies that support the learning of content and select those possessing the greatest leverage for success. The research voice offers one perspective. Students can successfully articulate instructional components that make a difference for them. When one contemplates relationships around instruction, students know what works for them. What do students want when it comes to this concept? Hear their voice and listen to their words.

Students say the best teachers:

Use effective practices, like hands-on projects. They keep up with the latest ideas.

19

NEWSFLASH: Students hate writing the answers to questions at the end of the chapter, sustained lectures without any discussion, and textbook-driven instruction!

Students do not enjoy classes where they are passive recipients of information. They want to be involved in their own learning. As students converse about their learning and instructional strategies that engage them, they may not use the terms, "best practices" or "research-based practices." However, they can effectively articulate what happens in classes where they learn best. One of the most frequent descriptors students use to describe these types of classes is the use of *"hands-on activities."* Students also seem to have an intuitive sense learning is a social activity ranking *group work* and being able to *"talk"* about what they are studying as being important characteristics of effective teaching. Additional strategies reflect the importance of different learning styles. Students enjoy classes characterized by the purposeful use of strategies such as:

- Projects
- Use of games for learning and review
- Experiments and labs
- Use of visual aids
- Class discussions related to real-life
- Use of manipulatives

It is also evident from listening to students that effective teachers plan for success. According to students, these teachers provide clear explanations and expectations. They guide students through the process. Effective teachers plan what happens during each phase of the teaching and learning process.

If students were asked, how would they describe the types of instructional activities YOU or others at YOUR SCHOOL use?

Students say the best teachers:

Use technology and find ways we can use our own technology at school in appropriate ways.

20

Students are avid users of technology and are confused when they attend schools where the adults don't recognize its value and power. Use of the computer as a tool for learning is a theme that resonates with all students. The motivational aspect, and the ability to create products depicting their learning is one of the major advantages students cite when encouraging teachers to incorporate the use of technology. Visits to classrooms and observations of student use of technology provide a rich repertoire of uses and engagement by students. Listening as primary students discuss the research they conducted while writing and producing their podcasts, one is amazed at the complexity of the task, the integration of skills, the problem solving and sense of accomplishment that accompanies their description.

Not only does technology offer the opportunity to use it as a tool, but it can also function as a delivery mode where instruction is more aligned to the needs of the learner. These needs can be defined in multiple ways including academic needs, interests of students, and even various forms of presentation based on how individual students learn best. It holds promise for educators and students. In the book, *Disrupting Class,* the author maintains, "Student-centric technology will make it affordable, convenient, and simple for many more students to learn in ways that are customized for them" (Christiansen, 2008, p. 92). When one contemplates the idea of aligning instruction to the learner, educators must recognize that today's students can be described as media multi-taskers. They spend around "6.5 hours a day" beyond the school day involved in media activity. Curwood (2009) shares "93 percent of youth ages 12 to 17 go online" with 55% using "social networking sites" (pp. 52-53). Customizing learning via technology begins by planning, not banning it as students walk through our doors.

How are YOU or YOUR SCHOOL promoting student use of technology to improve student learning?

Students say the best teachers:

Give meaningful work.
They know we do not like word searches, worksheets, or busy work.

21

This probably does not come as any great surprise but students detest what they repeatedly term as "busywork" in their classes. Fairly or unfairly, students equate worksheets with busywork. They also equate busywork with teachers who are not truly there to teach, but just "there for the money." Students feel strongly about this issue. Busywork is one of the primary reasons students cite as to why they dislike certain classes in schools.

The concept of busywork extends not only to assignments given during class, but also to homework tasks. Quantity versus quality is an argument often postulated for disdain of homework assignments. Students and parents question the necessity of doing 75 problems when 10 or 15 may provide evidence of student learning. In the book, *Rethinking Homework: Best Practices that Support Diverse Needs*, Cathy Vatterott initiates a discussion about the research related to homework. She provides recommendations for effective homework practices. According to Vatterott (2009), effective homework is definitely not busy work. It is predicated on recommended practices emanating from research, which includes careful consideration of the purpose of the homework task and the type of learning desired (pp, 96-99). She reiterates the perspective students emphatically voice, citing the work of Past (2006):

> Students do not often complete homework simply because the task is not meaningful. The most egregious homework practice is to assign busywork or tasks of dubious academic value that do not reinforce existing knowledge or demonstrate a mastery of knowledge (p. 100).

Even though busywork may be well-intentioned, it is seldom well-designed. It is evident the concept of busywork not only strikes a chord with students and their desire for meaningful tasks, but also in educational literature suggesting schools should reflect thoughtfully about the work students are asked to engage in on a consistent and systematic basis in schools.

If you were a student at your school, how would you describe the work YOU or others at YOUR SCHOOL require or assign?

Students say the best teachers:

Are energetic, enthusiastic, and enjoy their job.

22

When students talk about what makes a great teacher, they do so with great excitement and appreciation. Invariably, students share their best educators enjoy teaching and are enthusiastic. Students report they will take more difficult classes or even classes they dislike based on a teacher's zest for teaching. They use phrases such as the following:

- Loves kids and loves learning
- Works tirelessly for students
- Makes the entire class feel like they were good in math
- Is demanding and cares so much she almost strokes out
- Gives me confidence
- Helps me to become better with school by sharing their passion and expertise
- Lives, breathes and loves their content
- Makes me feel good about learning and makes me feel good about myself
- Makes me think, teaches lessons for life, not just class, inspires me

As one peruses these ideas, it might initially appear these students are expecting "SUPER TEACHER" with powers that can make the mundane exciting, the chronically disengaged motivated, or the downtrodden, empowered. However, that is not the case. What is awe-inspiring as students describe effective teachers is the respect and gratitude students articulate for these role models. Their words depict an appreciation for the authenticity of the instructor and the creation of an atmosphere of mutual respect. Students are aware of the roles teachers play in helping students succeed. They want teachers with high expectations or teachers who take the time to talk with them, sharing a positive view about what students can do or be. These teachers could not hide their love of education and learning if they tried. They take ownership of students, they take responsibility for presenting their love of content in an engaging way, but most of all they convey in words and actions, *I want to be here and I'm here for you!*

Are YOU or others at YOUR SCHOOL enthusiastic and energetic about teaching? Are you there for the students?

Students say the best teachers:

Help us beyond the school day or on their own time with our work.

23

One of the predominant themes emerging from the voices of students is the significance students attach to teachers and school staff who take their personal time to help them. Students are cognizant these teachers understand not every student easily grasps a concept. They are also cognizant of teachers taking time beyond the school day or during the day to help them. They are acutely aware these teachers are making a personal sacrifice for them. Students noted, "Before school, after school or whatever a student needed," - good teachers make learning accessible to all and success a probable outcome by providing additional assistance.

- The teacher doesn't yell when you are the only one who does not understand something. Instead, the teacher takes you aside and helps you understand.
- If they take time out of their busy day to take care of me then they will get my respect. One time I was failing a class, so the teacher took time out of their day to stay after school and help me improve my grade. It worked!!!!

Although students primarily discussed academic assistance, there were also those who suggested teachers assisted them with personal issues or problems, whether it was just listening and encouraging or whether it involved running the gauntlet of removing obstacles and finding resources for them. Some of the acts described were simple: taking time to listen, checking on a schedule change, or being sensitive about the desks in classrooms that called undue attention to an overweight student in front of her peers.

Students equate the willingness of a teacher to come in early and to stay late, to take his or her planning or lunch time to help me with a caring attitude. This affirms learning is intricately intertwined with caring for many students. One must gauge outcomes in the classroom with the following benchmark: "Only when learning occurs, can we be satisfied with our teaching efforts." Our responsibility as educators is learning by all. Students express deep gratitude to those teachers who help them on their own time.

How often do YOU or others at YOUR SCHOOL make time within the school day or beyond the school day to improve student learning?

Students say the best teachers:

Are in control of the class.

24

It is common for teachers to want students to like their class and to like them personally. Students truly value and respect a teacher who excels in classroom management which encompasses everything from outlining a well designed behavior management plan to the planning and preparation of instructional experiences. It even includes the effective use of instructional time. In an article entitled, *What Helps Students Learn*, classroom management was identified as one of the most important corollaries for student achievement (Wang, et al, 1994, pp. 74-79). When students talk about classroom management, they share things similar to the following. Effective teachers have order in class, have structure, create a positive environment, and treat everyone fairly. In contrast, they will share in classes they dislike, one of attributes often responsible for this classification relates to management. One eighth grader stated his dislike of a class:

🗣 "The teacher has no control. She has cried in class!"

This represents a stark contrast to what the research suggests students need and want. In an article by professors from the University of Memphis, the research of J.J. Irvine is cited emphasizing, "Students defined caring teachers as those who set limits, provided structure, held high expectations and expected them to succeed "(Thompson, Greer, & Greer, 2004, p. 6). Students need limits and structure. They need to know class operates with well-defined routines that are consistently and fairly enforced. In a report which shared the perspective of high school drop-outs, "Thirty-eight percent believed they had too much freedom and not enough rules" (Bridgeland, et al, 2006, p. iv). As Harry Wong suggests, the first two weeks of schools is key in setting the tone for the remainder of the year with the teacher truly being in control. Students do not function well and learning is jeopardized in chaotic classrooms.

How would students describe classroom management in YOUR classroom or the other classrooms in YOUR SCHOOL?

The Lesson for Educators

Students may not be aware of the complexity of planning educational experiences. However, they do know what works for them and what they esteem in effective classrooms. There are multiple resources providing guidance for professionals about instructional strategies, which when implemented with fidelity, can improve student achievement. Instructional strategies are the backbone of the teaching and learning process. David Berliner reminds everyone, "Teachers not armed with effective instruction cost students 20% per year in achievement" (Tileston & Darling, 2008, p.23). It is a task educators must constantly pursue with intentionality.

How does the student voice compare with the research voice? Initial comparisons seemingly do not show much alignment, if one is considering the exact descriptors used to depict practices between the research voice and the student voice. However, one could surmise that hands-on learning and research based practices are comparable, especially with the footnote that students believed teachers should remain current with their practices. At first glance, this may seem the only area of agreement. That conclusion would be erroneous. For example, as one considers meaningful work under the student voice, a case could be made that work and assignments become meaningful if students are actively engaged, emotionally engaged, and if there are opportunities for choice. Another similarity between the research voice and the student voice is the provision for additional support and individual help for students.

A second observation from comparison of the voices suggests that personality characteristics of the teacher and technology are more important to students than one might think. Continually, students use the term *enthusiastic* as an important variable during instruction. Students also hailed the importance of technology in their lives outside of schools and would like

116

to see schools value and utilize technology. The following graphic organizer offers an opportunity to compare and contrast the research voice and the student voice.

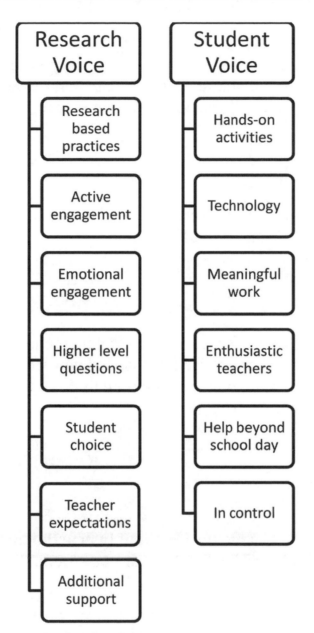

The Lesson for Educators

We need to have high expectations of ourselves and our students. We need to systematically incorporate the most effective and engaging instructional practices when presenting lessons.

A Trip Down Memory Lane Reflection

Continue to reflect on your history as a learner. The following questions related to instruction were developed as a guide.

1. Recall a time when your teacher or college professor provided choice on assignments or assessments. How did you make your decision about what to do and how did it make you feel? Did you feel more ownership for these assignments than times when choice was not given?

2. Can you think of a time you were frustrated by the work you were assigned by a teacher? What caused this frustration?

3. Hopefully, everyone has a special teacher in their educational experience. Was there ever a teacher or coach that helped you after school or beyond the regular day? What emotions are connected to those times? Did you work harder for this person?

Record any ideas from your memories about instruction around relationships that are meaningful and could apply to your classroom.

_____

_____

_____

_____

_____

_____

Professional Reflection

In my school:

Questions were listed at the end of each student voice description. After looking at these questions or reviewing the graphic organizer depicting the research and the student voice, think about what your school does well and what would be areas for improvement. Identify one or two areas of strength for your school and place in the appropriate column. Identify one or two areas you would like for your school to investigate.

Areas of strength at my school:	Areas I wish my school would target:

In my classroom:

As you think about the ideas presented in this chapter, identify what was especially meaningful for you. What are one or two ideas you would make a commitment to doing in your class? Write these three ideas in the space below.

I commit to doing the following things in my school or classroom:

Notes

Chapter 5

Relationships Around Assessment

Optimism is the faith that leads to achievement; nothing can be done without hope and confidence.

-Helen Keller

Relationships Around Assessment Research Voice

Assessment is one of the most utilized terms in educational lexicon. Some dismiss its importance. Some champion its informative value. Some see it as a necessary evil. As educators think about assessment, the guiding question becomes, "How do we ensure student success?" Measuring student success translates into using a variety of assessments to determine what students know and are able to do. Relationships around assessment view the learner and the learning as the primary concern, not the grade. Assessment exists for the student, as well as the teacher. One intently maximizes opportunities for student success and assessment becomes the process utilized to see progress in the journey of true learning.

When one cogitates on relationships around assessment, one might initially react with the assertion, assessment should be an objective informant about student learning. However, no area has more potential for violating the philosophy, do no harm. Students internalize assessment results. Many students equate assessment outcomes with their ability to learn and pursue more complex tasks. Even more disconcerting is the possibility of students utilizing assessments as indicators of how they see themselves, often leading to a sense of hopelessness and the tendency to give up. The ironic reality is assessments have the power to motivate students when utilized effectively. Relationships around assessment have some key components as depicted in the following chart.

Relationships

Around

Success on *first* assessment

Strategic interventions & enrichment

Entry points & goal setting

How will we ensure student success?

Self-assessment

Frequent formative assessments

Specific feedback

Assessment

One of the things schools may be unaware of is the major importance that hinges on the *first assessment of the year*. Tom Guskey (2008), educational researcher and author, makes a compelling argument that the first assessment sets the stage for future performance. The grade on the first assessment becomes a self-fulfilling prophecy for students connoting the importance of setting students up for success. Guskey recounts evidence from empirical studies suggesting the grade on the first assessment not only has a high correlation with the final grade, it also influences students' thought processes and how they perceive their success in a particular class. Think about this idea for a moment. As educators, we are successful adults. When we experience difficulty in completing a task or if we receive an unsatisfactory evaluation, what is our reaction? If we are honest with ourselves, we will admit not being motivated by failure. We wonder how others perceive and judge our abilities. We worry about being labeled by others. We may even attempt to hide or rationalize the unsuccessful outcome. If we can admit to doing this as adults, imagine what students may be thinking.

Students often judge themselves by not only the results of their assessment, but by their teachers' behaviors. Shirley Clarke (2005), an associate at the University of London, reminds professionals that the following practices send a powerful message to students and perpetuate a sense of failure and lack of belief in their own abilities. These include: "teacher's tone of voice; body language; how difficulty with learning is talked about; the over-use of teaching assistants with certain children; and the words used by teachers when interacting with children" (p. 85). Unfortunately, there are those within our profession who announce on the first day of class, "Half of you will fail". These teachers justify this message by stating and alluding to their status as a teacher with high standards and an unwillingness to compromise rigor. Those who espouse the goal to fail many of their students abdicate their responsibility to utilize more effective instructional techniques and teach their students. Unfortunately, assessments which render students vulnerable and hopeless are a badge of pride for some. Relationships around assessment do not embrace that view. Relationships around assessment embrace learning, which occurs at different rates and in different ways for all students.

Assessments lend themselves to a variety of uses. As one thinks about assessments and how they can be utilized throughout the learning process, there are a number of practices professionals can incorporate. Assessments provide educators with information they can utilize to plan ways to engage students in new learning. Having evidence of what students know offers educators *entry points* into the curriculum, an important consideration in curricular planning. One can also use *goal-setting by* the students as a way to involve students in the assessment process. "Students should identify some of their own learning goals" (Marzano, 2007, p. 23). In this context, students identify an area of interest within the content being studied, and identify an outcome (goal) related to the content. Other teachers involve students throughout the assessment process by employing targets and charts where students track their own progress on varied assessments enabling them to have a visual representation of their progress. This is an outcome shared by educational researchers Stiggins, Arter, Chappius, and Chappius (2004) who believe students should have a place at the assessment table. They advocate involving "students in assessing, tracking, and setting goals for their own learning" (p. 27). Students should not be viewed as silent partners in the assessment process.

There are a variety of assessments utilized by schools. *Frequent formative assessments* hold great promise for improving student achievement. Relationships around assessment suggest a focus on learning and the use of assessments *for* learning. This is especially true for children of poverty. "Underachieving children of poverty will experience an increase in their achievement scores when given the opportunity to learn in an environment focused on assessment for learning" (Barr & Parrett, 2007, p. 173). Fisher and Frey (2007) describe formative assessments as "ongoing assessments, reviews, and observations in a classroom" with the purpose of modifying or adapting instruction based on these frequent learning checks (p. 4). Ann Davies

(2007) in article entitled, "Involving Students in the Classroom Assessment Process" suggests formative assessments "impact learning- not merely a measure of what was learned. Using assessment in this way leads to greater socioeconomic, professional and personal success for students" (p. 32).

Many studies have been conducted conveying the impact of *frequent formative assessments*. One referenced in multiple intervention and assessment literature involves a meta-analysis conducted by Fuchs and Fuchs (1986) who shared that classrooms where there were two formative assessments a week resulted in a percentile gain of thirty points. Davies (2007) also touts the promise associated with the use of formative assessments conveying research which noted gains in achievement were so considerable, it was "found to be amongst the largest ever reported for educational interventions" (p. 32). The opportunity to gauge student understanding throughout the learning process using an early and often philosophy enables more students to experience success in the classroom. This is a process which is more motivational for students.

Visualize a paper with one of the following on it: *Needs Work! Good Paper! 80%,* a *checkmark* on the paper. How does this type of feedback help you as a learner? Yet, these are often representative of the only feedback students receive in some classes. A corollary to frequent formative assessments is the utilization of *specific feedback* to students. Specific feedback which is descriptive in nature provides students with guidance throughout the learning process. Davies (2007) provides an overview of specific, descriptive feedback. She writes:

> Specific, descriptive feedback is needed both during and after the learning. It is formative. In this kind of feedback, student work is compared to criteria, rubrics, models, exemplars, samples, or descriptions of excellence. Students learn what elements of their work (products, processes, or presentations) meet quality expectations and where they need to learn more and improve their work. Students understand this feedback more readily because it relates directly to their learning (p.32).

This feedback can include progress toward goals, questions guiding or cueing the learner or asking the learner to elaborate on ideas, comments redirecting the learning and even offering specific praise about a particular aspect of the work, when appropriate. Black, et al (2003) describes a study where students were provided with three different forms of feedback. Their goal was to answer the question, what type of feedback has the greatest influence on student learning? Three groups of students received different forms of feedback: (1) a grade, (2) comments, and (3) a combination of grade and comments. The results of the study revealed "learning gains were greatest for the group given only comments, with the other two treatments showing no gains" (p. 43). When students were presented with grades and comments, they focused primarily on the grade. Students receiving comments can "zero in" on what their next steps should be and how to improve their work. Marzano (2007) guides educators with two criteria for offering encouraging feedback. Although these two criteria relate to placing a grade on a paper, one can extrapolate and use these findings to structure comments in responding to students' work. They include:

> First, feedback must provide students with a way to interpret scores [or comments] in a manner that does not imply failure…Second, feedback must realize that effort on their part results in more learning (p. 105).

Decreasing evaluative assessments and feedback while increasing descriptive feedback enhances student achievement. Specific, descriptive feedback, especially within the framework of formative assessments connotes opportunities for improvement and is perhaps the most underused and misused tool educators have within their professional arsenal. When used as prescribed, it holds the promise of having a tremendous impact on student learning.

One aspect of assessment that is often neglected is *self-assessment*. Self assessment and reflection on the part of the learners enable them to help monitor their own learning. How often do lessons progress with little time devoted to closure or even no time carved out for student reflection? Students need the opportunity to process ideas and to make sense of content. Self-assessment tools afford this opportunity. This can be coupled with the practice of student goal setting, as well as students charting their own progress. There are multiple strategies teachers can utilize to facilitate this process. The first hurdle is ensuring self-assessment finds its way in every classroom.

> Research shows that when students are involved in the assessment process – by constructing the criteria by which they are assessed, self-assessing in relation to the criteria, giving themselves information to guide (or 'feed-forward' their learning), collecting and presenting evidence of their learning and reflecting on their strengths and needs – they learn more, achieve at higher levels, and are more motivated (Davies, 2007, pp. 31-32).

Reflection and self-assessment are no longer negotiable parts of a lesson. It is incumbent on those in education to find ways to systematically incorporate more student involvement and ownership in the assessment process.

Finally, as one considers relationships around assessment, we must be deliberate in our efforts to provide *strategic interventions and enrichment*. Learning does not stop with formative assessments. Richard DuFour and Becky Dufour (2006) crafted four questions about our efforts in schools. They are:

(1) What is it we want students to learn?

(2) How will we know when each student has learned it?

(3) How will we (the school) respond when some students don't learn?

(4) What is our response if they already know it?

It is incumbent on educators to provide strategic interventions and enrichment in their quest to address the last two questions. When some students don't learn, they need to know a safety net exists for them. They should be confident the teacher and school will intervene and work with

128

them if they do not demonstrate mastery on an assessment. Imagine the security of knowing a safety net exists for me, a student in this school. John Maxwell shares a story from Lloyd Ogilvie about a young circus performer who was a trapeze artist. The story offers educators with a vivid metaphor for thinking about safety nets for students. He shares:

> Once you know that the net below will catch you, you stop worrying about falling. You actually learn to fall successfully! What that means is, you can concentrate on catching the trapeze swinging toward you, and not on falling, because repeated falls in the past have convinced you that the net is strong and reliable when you do fall....The result of falling and being caught by the net is a mysterious confidence and daring on the trapeze. You fall less. Each fall makes you able to risk more. (Maxwell, 2001, p. 60)

Guskey (2007) in a compilation of articles edited by Douglas Reeves, one of the leading experts on assessments in education, advocates assessments being followed up with "high quality corrective instruction," as well as giving "students second chances to demonstrate success" (p.16). When this is the practice in classrooms and schools, students know that the schools believe in them. Schools need to be diligent in their efforts to create a culture of learning by believing in all students. By the same token, as we reflect on our diverse learners, providing enrichment or differentiated activities for those students who already know the information becomes an increasingly important component of instructional planning.

Students Speak: What Our Customers Say

Students should be perceived as active partners in each stage of the educational process. Often, the only role students assume in the assessment process is as the recipient of a grade or a comment about the quality of their work or their efforts. When this description characterizes what happens in the classroom, schools and teachers have lost the opportunity to use assessment to inform the learning process, and even negated opportunities for students to understand their role in the assessment. The research voice offers educators with detailed guidance about the use of assessment in the learning process. While students may not be mindful of the scope of educational research as it relates to assessment, they have ideas about what matters to them. What do students want when it comes to this concept? Hear their voice and listen to their words.

Notes

Students say the best teachers:

Tell us how we did on our work (timely & specific).

25

- "Figure it out on your own!"

- "You ask too many questions."

- "My teacher read my essay out loud in class as a reference on what *not* to do when writing which was humiliating and caused me to lose respect for that teacher."

- "The teacher told me in front of the class that my book was trash and that my opinion on the *Twilight Saga* didn't matter."

These are examples of some of the memorable comments students have received about their work in school. They are non-examples of what students perceive as effective feedback. If the goal of feedback is to help improve student learning, comments these students received were more indicative of feedback mirroring personal attacks and even having a detrimental impact than helping students know how to improve. Students simply give up. Some students even reported putting derogatory comments within the content of their homework to see if teachers read their work. Their hypothesis, "Our papers are not being read" was an accurate one.

In addition, students desire feedback in a timely manner. Sadly, some students report never receiving any of their work back. Students do work, turn it in to the teacher, and then the work seems to disappear in a dark abyss never to be seen again. Students report being frustrated when they rarely receive feedback or even when they just receive a checkmark at the top of their paper. When this occurs, students do not view the work they do as meaningful, nor do they interpret the teacher as caring about their work or about them. Students respect those teachers who take the time to respond to their assignments, and give feedback about how they can improve.

What type of feedback do YOU or others at YOUR SCHOOL give? Is it timely and meaningful? Is it about a grade or about learning?

Students say the best teachers:

Value our work and effort.

26

What messages do we convey with assessments, appraisals of student work, grades, and comments? If the goal is learning, do assessments reflect this? Do we value the effort and work of students? A teacher's words and comments are interpreted on such a personal level. They have a direct impact on how students view themselves and their ability to be successful in an educational setting. Consider the following incident shared by a student and ask yourself the question: "Could this happen in my school or district?"

> *As an avid poetry writer, I found an outlet for my emotions. During an assignment, we were supposed to construct a poem to the tune of our favorite song. I had always been complimented on my poetry so I did not expect it when my teacher read my poem and promptly asked me, "What is this garbage?"*
>
> *I don't think she realized until that moment that I had written it, but I promptly tore it to shreds, told her to give me an F on the assignment and said I would never write a poem again. I lost my love for it, and haven't written one since.*

The power of our words – do we realize how students interpret them? Often times, off-the-cuff remarks are made about a piece of work or a performance on an assignment. The intent of the comment does not match the impact of it. As educators, it is our responsibility to always protect the dignity of the learner. If a student's work is demeaned, especially in front of their peers, we have not only devalued the work and effort of the student, we have violated one of our roles as educators: improving student learning and communicating our belief in each child. What if you were this child? What if you were the parent of this young lady?

We are not suggesting educators mislead students about the quality of their work. We are sharing there are appropriate ways for providing feedback which can motivate students to improve. However, it starts by valuing the work and effort of students.

What assurances are in place for students that YOU or others at YOUR SCHOOL value their work and effort?

Students say the best teachers:

Tell us they believe in us and work with us to be successful.

27

It's been said that the leader should be a dealer in hope. Classroom teachers, as leaders in their respective classrooms, must be dealers in hope for the students they teach. Often students see and feel the content is beyond their grasp. "I'm not smart enough." "I can't do that." "Everybody else seems to understand but me." These statements reflect the tendency learners have to give up and not persevere with a task or assignment. They do not view themselves as capable.

We do not teach in utopian classrooms with all students having the background knowledge, the same skills sets in literacy, numeracy, and reasoning which translates to success for all students during the initial instruction. We teach in classrooms with individual students. Students need to know you believe in them. As adults, most of us can recall two different types of classrooms we experienced as students. There was that classroom where a teacher sparked an interest in challenging content and conveyed by their interactions with us, we would be successful. Then, there is that other classroom where teachers took great pride announcing that a percentage of the students would fail. Which class did we prefer? Students in our classrooms mirror our preference. We want to be where someone wants us to succeed.

All students need to know we believe in them and will work to help them be successful. However, it is especially important for struggling students. A powerful reminder that grounds us to the reality of some of our students is a quote from a presentation given by Dr. Roger Cleveland, an assistant professor: "Few realize the courage it takes to return to a place where he/she failed yesterday, the day before, and in all probability will fail again the next day." Would we be able to match the courage of these learners? Students have tremendous respect for educators who believe in their abilities and are willing to find ways to help them succeed.

What are some examples demonstrating that YOU or others at YOUR SCHOOL believe in all students and will help them be successful?

The Lesson for Educators

Assessment garners much attention and discussion. There are volumes of educational literature distinguishing between testing and assessment, detailing the important role assessment plays in learning, and providing professionals with blueprints for more effective use of assessments in the learning process. Assessment literacy is a vital area of professional knowledge and growth for teachers. Assessment literacy is also a vital aspect in promoting not only student achievement, but positive relationships in schools. Tom Hierck (2009), an assistant superintendent and former member of the Ministry of Education in British Columbia, shares a quote by Rick Stiggins depicting the power of assessments on relationships in schools: "You can enhance or destroy students' desire to succeed in school more quickly and permanently through your use of assessment than with any other tools you have at your disposal" (p. 245). Hierck continues his explanation noting, "Assessment is particularly reliant upon the establishment and cultivation of positive and effective relationships" (p. 245).

Comparisons between the research voice and the student voice underscore the potential relationships around assessment have for improving student achievement. However, it is also a testament to the fragile nature of those relationships, with students being able to recount experiences and stories where their love for an activity, such as writing or their passion for a content is lost forever because of the type of feedback they received from a teacher. Hierck (2009) reminds readers about the delicate nature that exists around assessments and relationships citing the research of Daniel Goleman which focused on at-risk students. Goleman found:

> "… that those placed with cold or controlling teachers struggled academically – regardless of whether their teachers followed pedagogic guidelines for good instruction. But if these students had a warm and responsive teacher, they flourished and learned as well as other kids. These stunning results show that quality of relationship above all else is the springboard to success" (p. 246)

As schools, we are charged with the responsibility of success for all students. What is the take-away message from the research and from the student voice? Relationships around assessment can either foster student success or inhibit it. We need to utilize the research voice and the student voice to foster success!

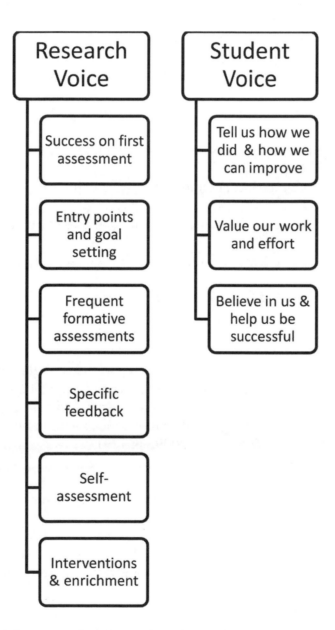

Comparison of the research voice and student voice suggests students should not be passive recipients of information about their work in schools. Classroom leaders must ask themselves, what roles can students play and how can we involve them as partners in their own education? Schools that have delineated a process and have focused their efforts on clarifying that process experience more success. Students who are knowledgeable about their performance and what they can do to mediate the difference between expectations and current performance with supportive teachers have greater likelihood for success and a decreased possibility they will become one of the thirty-five percent (35%) of students who drop out of school due to failing in school. The perspective of high school dropouts is captured in a report entitled, *The Silent Epidemic*. These students shared one of the pathways which might help students stay in school was to "improve instruction and access to support for struggling students." Among these dropouts, "70% believed more tutoring, summer school, and extra time with the teacher would have improved their chances of graduating" (Bridgeland, Dilulio, & Morison, 2006, pp. iv –v).

Beyond the dropout perspective, we must remember connections in classrooms are valuable in and of themselves. The book, *The High Performing School Benchmarking the 10 Indicators of Effectiveness*, reminds readers of that. The authors share the following research:

> Students who are connected with their schools report they are glad to attend school and enjoy it overall. This enjoyment adds to the diligence with which students perceive learning, the effort they exert on tasks and assignments, and their persistence in working through complex or difficult assignments, all of which result in increased learning and achievement" (Dunsworth & Billings, 2009, p. 129).

Student effort and persistence in working through difficult assignments are even more enhanced when relationships around assessment and practices from the research voice and the student voice are considered. Students offer educators with some common sense practices about what is important to them and where to start.

The Lesson for Educators

Students view assessments as value judgments, not only about their work but about themselves. Assessments are used by students to judge whether or not they will be successful in schools.

A Trip Down Memory Lane Reflection

Continue to reflect on your history as a learner. The following questions related to assessment experiences were developed as a guide.

1. Think of a time you were not successful on an assignment or test. When your received that grade, how did it make you feel? Was there ever a time when the teacher re-taught the material allowing you to redo the assignment or retake the test to demonstrate your learning? How did that make you feel about that class and the content you were learning?

2. In the majority of your learning experiences, do you believe the teacher placed the most emphasis on the grade or on the learning? What concerned you the most as a student?

3. What was the best feedback you ever received from a teacher that enabled you to understand a difficult concept or allowed you to demonstrate your learning?

4. Have you ever felt badly about yourself based on the results of an assessment? Has anyone every judged your ability by the results on a test? Describe your feelings and the efforts you put forth in that class.

Record any ideas from your memories about assessment experiences that you could apply to your classroom.

_____

_____

_____

_____

_____

Professional Reflection

In my school:

Questions were listed at the end of each student voice description. After looking at these questions or reviewing the graphic organizer depicting the research and the student voice, think about what your school does well and what would be some areas identified for improvement. Identify one or two areas of strength for your school and place in the appropriate column. Identify one or two areas you would like for your school to investigate.

Areas of strength at my school:	Areas I wish my school would target:

In my classroom:

As you think about the ideas presented in this chapter, identify what was especially meaningful for you. What are one or two ideas you would make a commitment to doing in your class? Write these ideas in the space below.

I commit to doing the following things in my school or classroom:

Notes

Chapter 6

Relationships Around Recovery

There is a certain degree of satisfaction in having the courage to admit one's errors. It not only clears the air of guilt and defensiveness, but often helps solve the problem created by the error.
-Dale Carnegie

Never ruin an apology with an excuse.
-Kimberly Johnson

Relationships Around Recovery Research Voice

Words are so powerful! Words, when used to demean and discourage others, are often the first line of defense when individuals feel threatened, unsure, frustrated, or just in a hurry and not thinking about what comes from within. Words, when used to celebrate and encourage others, can evoke positive emotions that will last for days. Unfortunately, these words sometimes remain unspoken because, in the course of day-to-day interactions, we seldom make time in our schedules to share what we appreciate in others. However, there are times when words need to be shared reflecting the times we have prematurely judged someone without having all the facts or when we uttered phrases which are not truly representative of who we are personally or professionally.

Mistakes are a part of one's life. If a person was granted with the power of a "do over," is there any individual who can boast he would have never chosen words and actions more carefully? Relationships are more fragile than we like to believe. As individuals, we often underestimate the seemingly benign words and actions derailing relationships. We are quick to place blame and, most would surmise, reticent to acknowledge the times we said or did things that would never make it on the pages of our professional brag book. It is a given – all are human and each person makes mistakes. Even with that being a known variable, it is still a difficult task to first, get individuals to admit they made a mistake, and second, to use two simple words that make all the difference – *I'm sorry*.

As one thinks about mistakes and how those mistakes translate to the interactions schools have within their walls, it is evident schools should borrow some of the practices and expectations found in business and leadership literature. There is nothing mysterious about these practices. They simply point one in the right direction about their interactions, whether the type of relationship is student to student, teacher to student, teacher to teacher, administrator to teacher, or teacher to parent.   It might be advantageous to recall an adage which basically states, "We want to be judged by our intentions; but we often judge others by their actions." The following graphic organizer provides an overview of the art of recovery and the elements that make it meaningful.

Typically, one will not hear discussions in schools or in professional development about experiences that include learning how to recover from a mistake. Yet, it is one of the keys to maintaining effective relationships in any capacity, personal or professional. Ken Blanchard and Margret McBride (2003), authors of the *One Minute Apology* maintain an apology begins with surrender and ends with integrity. Surrender is basically acknowledging you acted or behaved inappropriately and, with a *sense of urgency*, make amends to the ones you hurt. It is the act of apologizing. Integrity is an opportunity for a person to reflect on his own behavior, forgiving oneself, and making a commitment to ensure the behavior doesn't occur again. The ability to admit one has erred requires one be sincere, genuine, and honest. It is an uncomfortable act, this act of surrender and this act of integrity. It is also an act that is necessary to move beyond the mistake.

It is our contention that adults in school are nurturing people who are in a profession because they care about students and they want to make a positive difference in their lives. One would hope there would never be a need for apologies in the schools and classrooms. The reality is mistakes are a part of our lives. When mistakes result in someone being hurt by our words or deeds, it requires action. That action begins with an apology. Students are sensitive to how the adults in a school interact with them. Whether it is through inappropriate body language, sarcasm, or the words used, mistakes occur in our interactions with others. Those mistakes impact not only the way students view their teachers, it also impacts how students view themselves. As one surveys the literature related to mistakes, there are common attributes associated with good apologies.

Apologize quickly! The more immediate an apology, the better it is for everyone involved. Those who have been injured by our words or actions tend to believe the motive behind an immediate apology is more genuine. Generally, if one can apologize within twenty-four hours, it makes a big difference in how the apology is perceived. The longer one goes before making an apology, the more others tend to view the apology with a sense of skepticism. The offended party starts to believe the apology is motivated by some other reason than to make amends for one's mistakes. As Blanchard and McBride (2003) share, "The longer you wait to apologize, the sooner your weakness is perceived as wickedness" (p. 26).

An apology must be *sincere and empathetic*. Most people, especially students, can read between the lines and discern when one is truly sorry for what occurred. Look at the situation from the other person's point of view. How would you feel? When you acknowledge the hurt or damage done, "you are validating their feelings and the recipient begins to sense that you understand the situation. This is important to rebuilding your relationship because it legitimizes their reaction…" (Perfect Apology, 2009, p. 2). When one makes a mistake and an apology is necessary, it is imperative we recognize the apology is not about us, it is about the injured party. Knowing this, one should not attempt to justify or defend their actions. This is difficult because it is human nature to try to explain. Others interpret these justifications as an unwillingness to take responsibility for our actions. Please don't begin your apology or use the following phrases in your apology: *If I did something* - or *I **may** have offended you*. Omit the words, "if" and "may." We should assume the infraction is a serious one that merits a genuine response and remember, it's about the other person!

An expectation often shared is one should learn from his mistakes. A part of learning from a mistake is *assuring others that the mistake will not be repeated*. This is a promise to the other individual we are cognizant of the error in judgment and will honor him by making sure the infraction will not occur again. This is a promise to oneself that self-control will be exercised and a commitment has been made to respond differently the next time. It both cases, we are taking responsibility for our words and actions. Repeating the same mistake means risking the relationship.

A fourth attribute of recovering from a mistake is to make sure the *apology equals the offense.* Suppose a teacher gets upset with a student and in front of the class, makes a negative remark about that student. What are the implications about the impending apology required in this situation? When the apology is given, it should be one that is shared in front of the class because the student was admonished and embarrassed in front of the class. Simply, taking the student aside and apologizing one-on-one is not enough, although a teacher could do both to truly communicate to the student a desire to rebuild or salvage the relationship.

The benchmark of an effective apology is *resolving an issue to the satisfaction of the injured party.* This entails the person accepting your apology and not holding the mistake against you. Take responsibility for your actions and share how badly you feel about the situation with words like terrible, ashamed, guilty, embarrassed, or even the phrase, let you down. You are attempting to share with the other person "you are suffering from your blunder. You are opening yourself up by showing the mistake had a bad effect on you. The other person becomes more….willing to discuss their feelings because you have expressed yours" (Earthling Communication, 2007, p. 2). After the apology, questions can be asked to determine if the issue has been resolved. What could I do to make this situation better? Is there anything else I can do or say to let you know that I am truly sorry for what happened? Do you feel the situation has been resolved to your satisfaction?

The final attribute of an apology is *adding an extra or personal touch to the apology.* This could take the form of many different things. Retail stores often offer coupons with an apology. One could send a follow-up note acknowledging the value of the relationship and the importance of the other person. A small, inexpensive gift might be sent to the individual to express appreciation for acceptance of your apology. If the injured party is a student, it might be a soft drink, lunch on me, or tickets to a school event. It could even be giving students a pencil or eraser as recognition that a mistake was made and a genuine hope the apology erased any hurt feelings. Although an authentic apology is enough, an extra or personal touch is an option that conveys one values the relationship.

"You are thought of more highly once you own a mistake because others will see you are human and have feelings…" (Barnerias, 200, p. 1). This sentiment is also shared by J.D. Powers in the book, *Satisfaction* who believes it may be better to make a mistake and recover well than to never make any mistakes at all (Denove & Powers, 2006). Mistakes offer opportunities for individuals to see who you truly are as a person, a company, or even an institution. This attests to the importance of every staff member being trained in and knowing how to recover from mistakes. At the heart of an apology, is trust. Can you re-establish trust by being remorseful and issuing an effective apology? The answer is, in the majority of cases, a sincere apology delivered appropriately can de-escalate a situation and result in individuals regaining elements of trust. Walt Whitman once said, "It takes a great deal of character and strength to apologize quickly out of one's heart rather than out of pity. A person must possess himself and have a deep sense of security in fundamental principles and values in order to genuinely apologize."

There are two nuances one needs to be aware of related to recovering from mistakes. Although a quick apology is the best apology, there may be times when a offended party is angry and needs a little time to calm down. A person must always read the situation with the goal of issuing an apology at the earliest possible moment. The second is a reminder that apologies are difficult for both parties. It may be advisable for one to take the time to think and plan an apology, possibly even scripting some of the dialogue if the situation calls for it. Face to face is always best, but if this is not possible, an apology over the phone is the next best option. Dale Carnegie, author of the book, *How to Win Friends and Influence People*, has been advising people since 1935, "When you're wrong, admit it quickly and emphatically" (p. 142). Perhaps, people need to refrain from looking at mistakes as obstacles and view them as opportunities – opportunities to showcase their character, honesty, and credibility. This is not only important when interacting with students, it is equally important in our interactions with colleagues, supervisors, and even in our personal relationships.

Students Speak: What Our Customers Say

There is guidance about how to recover from mistakes from an array of experts and references. Probably, few ever contemplate about recovering from mistakes with students. Students are passionate about the significance of relationships around recovery. For students, relationships around recovery is an issue of trust. Trust is fragile, but it is a crucial element in teacher-student relationships. As educators, we need to understand not only the importance of trust and how that is violated when mistakes are made with students, it is also a matter of respect for students, respect for who they are as individuals and respect for what they bring to the classroom. We need to understand that recovering from mistakes is an opportunity to model the values we espouse as meaningful character education traits and opportunities to rebuild trust. When one contemplates relationships around recovery, students value certain behaviors and dispositions from their teachers. What do students want when it comes to this concept? Hear their voice and listen to their words.

Notes

Students say the best teachers:

Admit it when they mess up or make mistakes.

28

Embarrassing a student in front of the class, using sarcasm inappropriately and in a way that demeans students, making derogatory comments when a student doesn't understand, intercepting a note or text and reading it aloud to the class, rolling one's eyes when a student responds to questions, sharing information about one student to another student, losing a paper a student handed in and holding it against them, accusing a student of an infraction they didn't commit, giving misinformation to a class –

These are examples of situations leading to misunderstandings in the classroom. No one likes to be embarrassed and students report simply shutting down in some of these scenarios.

While the acts and words may be inadvertent, the impact is not. One student reported she posed a question for clarification in language arts class. The teacher responded, "Wow, that sounds like another blonde question!" The student internalized the remark, "The teacher is saying I am dumb." She attended class the rest of the year, never asking another question. When these wrongdoings occur and the issue is never resolved, the relationship is forever severed and learning suffers.

In contrast to these scenarios, a teacher made some harsh remarks to a student. The next day, the teacher asked the student to remain after class. The student feared it was going to be more of the same, but the teacher looked at the student and shared, "I overreacted. I don't know why I responded that way. I am sorry for my words and for making you feel badly. Please forgive me." The result of that apology was a student who came to class, paid attention and was well-behaved the remainder of the year. When a teacher admits a mistake, students feel valued and important in that classroom. It's a transforming experience.

There is another slant students offered with regard to admitting one's mistakes. It was very meaningful to students when staff members shared, in an appropriate manner, mistakes they had made in their own lives. Hopefully, by sharing one's mistakes and the lessons learned, it can help our students avoid some of those same pitfalls.

Do YOU or others at YOUR SCHOOL admit mistakes to students?

Students say the best teachers:

Take up for us. They have the courage to stand up for us when we are treated unfairly.

29

We would all like to believe we have someone in our corner that not only believes in us, but has the courage to speak up in times we need them. Students know they are in a subordinate role in schools. They know they are in an environment with rules, expectations, and authority figures. However, they want to know the culture of a school is one which is principle-driven. This is when the adults are confident enough, and believe in the students enough, they would intervene on a student's behalf, especially if a student is in an embarrassing situation or even falsely accused of an infraction.

Some research refers to this characteristic as compassion. Even though all malicious and insensitive acts cannot be eliminated in schools, caring teachers can help manage and diminish its occurrence:

> Effective teachers are supportive of students in multiple ways and help them meet their needs for belonging and success. These teachers are remembered for noticing when children were left out of games on the playground and for taking action to prevent such things from happening. Such simple actions eliminated the embarrassment that many children have to face every day. And from our students' recollections, it was clear that such wise behavior was remembered vividly years later" (Thompson, Greer, & Greer, 2004, p. 6).

As human beings we all remember those times we have felt left out, been falsely accused, or had opportunities undermined by others.

There are multiple examples of how this could unfold in schools. Does a scholarship go to the deserving student or to a student popular with staff? When a teacher fails to put a student's grades in the computer system and a child shows up as ineligible at his first middle school basketball game, what happens? A student who is obese will have difficulty finding a seat in the classroom. Will anyone think ahead and ensure this student has an appropriate seat? One student makes a disparaging remark about a classmate, will the situation be addressed?

Would students say YOU or others at YOUR SCHOOL stand up for them, even if it involved intervening with fellow staff members?

157

The Lesson for Educators

Relationships around recovery might be an area educators tend to ignore or de-value, but that would be an oversight on our part. Schools are a microcosm of the world. With that in mind, everyone is required to negotiate various aspects of relationships within the workplace. Fundamental to the success of any endeavor is establishing an element of trust. Without trust, no one will be as successful as they could be, individually or collectively. Part of a trusting relationship is admitting to oneself when a mistake has occurred and being willing to apologize and work toward moving that relationship forward. It is important students learn tolerance and forgiveness. David Cottrell (2007), author and chief executive officer for Cornerstone Leadership Institute, remind readers that we should, "Practice forgiveness when the relationship is tested. Forgiveness is the oil of relationships" (p. 133). While our focus is on teacher and student relationship, this is a lesson important in any relationship context, even administrator to teacher, or vice versa.

Secondly, relationships around recovery exemplify the human element existing in schools. Life is not made up of just positive experiences. It is comprised of the good, the bad, and unfortunately, often the ugly. Conflicts occur. When they do, we must remember, "No relationship can strengthen and grow in an environment of negativity" (Cottrell, 2007, p. 133). Mistakes, oversights, and offenses are a part of life and to pretend they do not occur in educational settings is a missed opportunity. To ignore them is to ignore teachable moments. Beverly Engel (2001) in the book, *The Power of an Apology* offers the perspective that failure to admit mistakes and convey regret adds insult to injury and blatantly communicates disrespect to the injured party. If students do not learn about or witness adults modeling civility in the educational setting, where else are they going to learn the right thing to do whether they are on the giving or receiving end of situations requiring an apology. Engel (2001) specifies behaviors where an apology should be issued: putdowns, rude or inconsiderate behavior, sarcasm, thoughtlessness, impatience, disrespect, forgetfulness, unfairness, gossiping, lying about others, or just being mean-spirited in a particular situation. Contrition is a great teacher for the giver and the receiver.

Relationships without warranted apologies lead to resentment. No one likes to be unfairly treated and students have an innate sense of fairness. They know if fairness is consistently practiced in a classroom. They know if a classroom is a place characterized by respect for all students. They know if caring and effective teachers successfully address mistakes and conflicts. If situations are not resolved, many students will "rewind" or "replay" that situation over and over again. The negative feelings escalate, creating barriers in the classroom, and may even result with students becoming disengaged.

As one makes comparisons between the research voice and the student voice in the following graphic organizer, it is apparent that the research voice focuses on how to apologize while the student voice communicates the significance of the act to students. In addition, students hope when they are vulnerable because of a mistake, misinformation, or the potential of an embarrassing moment, educators will have the courage to stand up for them. The benefits of these acts extend well beyond the moment. Nelson Mandela once shared, "If you talk to a man in a language he understands, that goes to his head. If you talk to him in *his* language, that goes to his heart." Apologies are a language that goes to the heart and this appears to be why they are significant enough to become part of the student voice.

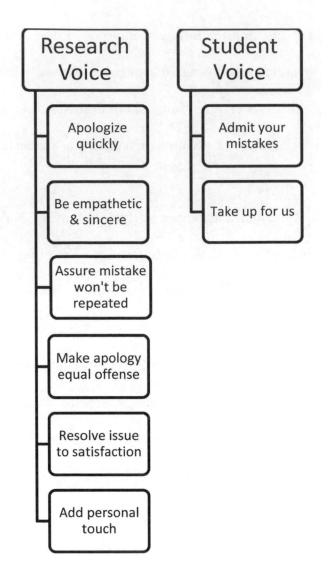

"A Carnegie study showed that 85 percent of a person's success was determined by what researchers called ability to deal with people and attitude" and even though knowledge and technical skills are important, it's the people skills that matter (Cottrell, 2007, p. 128). Educators must be willing to incorporate the ability to admit mistakes as one of those important people skills. The ability to do so is more indicative of the strength of their character than as a weakness. In the book, *In Our Own Words*, students share their perspectives about school. One of the themes emanating from their writing is the importance of human and humane interactions. "Student authors emphasize the ways in which they have felt such humanity missing in their interactions" in schools (Shultz & Cook-Sather, 2001, p. 4). Schools need to take advantage of opportunities that demonstrate the humanity in our interactions, especially if our actions have resulted in students feeling wronged or hurt.

The Lesson for Educators

We need to develop an awareness of our words and actions,
knowing when these result in offending or hurting students,
a sincere apology should be forthcoming.

A Trip Down Memory Lane Reflection

Continue to reflect on your history as a learner. The following questions related to recovery were developed as a guide.

1. Think of a time when a teacher made a mistake. Did that teacher admit it? How did you respond to the teacher's willingness or unwillingness to admit he/she made a mistake?

2. Has a teacher ever been sarcastic, embarrassed you, or devalued your contributions in a class? How did it make you feel? What could the teacher have done to recover? Did he? Describe how it impacted your efforts and your learning in that class.

3. Have you ever observed a teacher or administrator stand-up for you or another student when they were being mistreated? Have you ever observed an educator who remained silent or ignored a situation when a student was being degraded or was treated unjustly? Describe your reactions and how you felt about those teachers or administrators.

Record any ideas about relationships around recovery that you could apply to your classroom.

_____

_____

_____

_____

_____

_____

Professional Reflection

In my school:

Questions were listed at the end of each student voice description. After looking at these questions or reviewing the graphic organizer depicting the research and the student voice, think about what your school does well and what would be some areas identified for improvement. Identify an area of strength for your school and place in the appropriate column. Identify an area you would like for your school to investigate.

Areas of strength at my school:	Areas I wish my school would target:

In my classroom:

As you think about the ideas presented in this chapter, identify what was especially meaningful for you. What idea can you make a commitment to doing in your class? Write it in the space below.

I commit to doing the following things in my school or classroom:

Notes

Chapter 7

Relationships: From Black and White to Color

Life doesn't count for much unless you're willing to do your small part to leave our children – all our children – a better world. Even if it's difficult. Even if the work seems great. Even if we don't get very far in our lifetime.

-Barack Obama
Speech, June 15, 2008

Listening to the Student Voice

One way to begin thinking about existing practices is to consider the student view or student voice. How often do we seek the input and views of students? How often do we engage students in solving issues at the school? "Administrators and teachers who dismiss the importance of student perspective and its corollary, student input, miss the opportunity to create quality programs with students" (Gilbert & Robins, 1998, p. 15). As illustrated in previous chapters, students have insights about what promotes learning often paralleling the educational research. Students know what makes a difference for them and can articulate it very effectively. Robert Haden, in an essay entitled, "We Are Not Robots!" underscores the importance of teacher and student relationship.

> When teachers relate to students and make tiny inquiries, students feel more comfortable with the situation. At our school teachers are getting better at understanding teens who sit in desks before them, mostly because they've opened their ears and eyes a crack (Gilbert & Robins, 1998, p. 36).

Educators must do more than opening their ears and eyes a crack. They must enter into the relationship building business with eyes wide open. Students repeatedly voice their desire for teachers who come to know and understand who they are as individuals. They ache for a personal touch, for stories and examples in lessons, for making meaning, and for schools to see them as individuals.

In the children's book, *The Story of Ferdinand,* one of the themes that emanates from the pages is the concept of individuality. Ferdinand refused to play like all the other bulls. "He just liked to sit quietly and smell the flowers" in his favorite spot under a cork tree (Leaf, 1936, p. 8). No matter what happened or who talked to him, he remained committed to being who he was and what he wanted to be. Others could not coax him, not even his mother who worried about him.

No one ever asked Ferdinand why, they just tried to change his behavior. So many times in schools, it seems as if we never consider the perspective of all the Ferdinands. Gilbert and Robins (1998), authors of a book about how high school students perceive their school, emphasize the role of each individual student in the learning process. They write:

> …teachers need to consider that no matter how fancy a song, dance, or comedy routine they do in class, students individually decide to learn the song, dance, comedy, or the ideas in the lesson. The student has to agree to learn. It is easier to get meaningful agreement when students sense this control and act upon it.

The authors continue by sharing with readers how to promote learning in light of this individuality.

> There are two ways of accomplishing this goal. One is cognitive, in which the student consciously agrees that the assignment and lesson are meaningful and hence worth learning. The other is psychological and emotional. The student identifies with or enjoys the instructor or the assigned work. Learning may happen because of unconscious factors (p. 11).

As suggested in this description, either approach promotes learning. Traditionally, schools have relied primarily on the cognitive approach. One could probably assume few have reflected on this process. As we begin to think what might it might look like to think about learning from either of these approaches, two questions can guide our efforts.

(1) How do we make the learning meaningful to students; and

(2) How can we maximize the emotional and psychological connection to schools or to classes?

As one contemplates these questions, one of the immediate responses related to make learning meaningful is student application of knowledge and making learning relevant. Consideration of the second question leads to the obvious answer of an intentional focus on relationship building in schools. In so doing, we must see the individuals we are instructing. The commonality of a response for both questions is being student-centered. We must know our students.

Although relationships are important for all students, they are vital for students from poverty. Tileston and Darling (2008), authors and founders of educational and learning organizations write:

> For many students in poverty, relationships take precedence over almost everything else. It is the one thing that gives them ownership. When differentiating for content, it is important to note we must first build a relationship with students that has its premise that we are all learners together – including the teacher. It is not the curriculum and the teacher against the student; it is the student and teacher tackling the curriculum, and together they will be successful (p. 102).

Students need to know the teacher is their advocate, conveying the message; I'm in your corner. The power of a teacher in the lives of students and how they approach the teaching and learning process is the key variable in determining student success in school. While that statement is empowering, it is also conveys a level of accountability that is frightening. Assuming the role, "I am the determining factor in the classroom" is one requiring a commitment to student success. Researchers note that not only is learning impacted by the quality of the teacher relationship, but that student resiliency is also influenced by these relationships. In the book, *Why Culture Counts,* the authors share a comment from Bonnie Bernard that underscores this idea.

> A common finding in resilience research is the power of a teacher – often without realizing it – to tip the scale from risk to resilience…The bottom line and starting point for creating turnaround classrooms and schools that provide caring relationships, high expectations, and opportunities for participation is the deep belief on the part of teachers and school staff that every child and youth has innate resilience, the capacity for healthy development and successful learning (Tilestone & Darling, 2008, p. 163).

Tipping the scale from risk to resilience requires an in-depth knowledge of who the students are, what their situations are, and what they care about as individuals and as learners.

The Potential Relationships Offer

"We have to be interesting enough to gain their attention; we have to be passionate enough to strike love for the subject in their hearts; and we have to be human enough for them to connect with what we are saying" (Ridnouer, 2006, p. 80). These are the words of a math teacher of forty years who captured the magic of teaching and the magnitude of the task facing educators. Teaching begins with relationships. Our profession cannot continually negate the influence of relationships in the classroom by hoping positive relationships are established by all teachers. We would be deceiving ourselves. Showing up in a classroom to lecture ostensibly on content is not what a teacher does. Teaching and learning should be inseparable and should be predicated on relationship building and making connections in the classroom.

Relationships, even though they are often the neglected child in school improvement efforts, are correlated with many aspects of schooling. Relationships are a student achievement issue and research substantiates the impact on learning and closing the achievement gaps. Various references have been included throughout the pages of this book to elucidate the need for addressing relationships because of their impact on success in school.

Relationships are a school finance issue. Schools are generally funded on the basis of the number of students who are enrolled (membership) or attend school (attendance rate). When schools lose students, they lose dollars from their budgets. The straightforward nature of the nexus existing between relationships and finances needs little clarification other than consideration of the question, What are schools doing to meet the needs of the first customers in their schools? We need to be preparing for the day when students can decide where they want to attend classes because of the school choice movement. Would students choose your school?

Finally, relationships are also a school safety issue with the plea from many of those in the safe schools movement advocating the need for schools to develop relationships with students to combat the violence occurring in some schools. As one consults school safety literature, it is alarming to see the disconnect many students experienced at school resulting in all forms of violence, including the most feared, school shootings. Dr. Robert Brooks, a psychologist who has written about school safety, champions the significance of relationship building as a deterrent to school violence. He writes:

> Metal detectors, cameras, and similar devices provide some protection and that should not be minimized, but they fail to address what I consider to be the vital component of school safety and violence prevention, namely, the relationship that we develop and nourish with each student (Brooks, 2002, p.1).

Dr. Brooks has interviewed a number of students, many who were angry and lacked a sense of belonging at school. As he references some of these interviews, it is obvious the students are disillusioned by the relationships existing for them in schools. The comments from these students are chilling – chilling for how some students experience school and chilling to think how some adults at school glibly interact with students with little regard of how their words and action are being interpreted. Consider the following comments from a high school student who was discussing bullying:

> If only some of the teachers knew how they came across to us. Some are sarcastic. Don't say hello to you, and always assume you did something wrong. It's hard to take them seriously when they talk about kindness and respect (p. 1)

The student proceeded to share that when teachers care about students, they are more receptive to the message because they are "practicing what they preach." Dr. Brooks' (2002) insights and words about school violence and relationships are deafening in terms of the magnitude of their importance. "Research shows that a positive relationship with an adult who is available to provide support when needed is one of the most critical factors in preventing school violence"

170

(p. 2). This research requires schools and educators to take stock of existing practices, as well as initiate conversations about what we could do to develop connections with students. What planning efforts are being devoted to fostering positive relationships among all staff with all students in your school? Are you aware of how students perceive their interactions with the adults in their school? As Dr. Brooks and others cited in his work connote, sometimes it's the little things that count.

Relationships At Your School

As discussions ensue about schools and relationships, one should be prepared to hear responses that may sound similar to the following:

- That is not an issue at our school.
- We can't do that. Our job is to teach content. We can't assume responsibility for everything.
- We are already doing most of these things at our school.
- When are we going to stop spoon-feeding these students? It's time our students understand how it is in the real world.
- I don't get paid to do that relationship thing.

Have you heard similar comments when discussing changes that need to be made related to school improvement? There will be a few within our profession who always subscribe to finding fault with any efforts. However, the majority of those within our profession chose to become teachers because they personally experienced the power of someone who believed in them. The challenge becomes not only finding ways to make it happen in your school, but also finding ways to make it happen for every child.

What if one were to develop a litmus test for relationships in school? What might it look like? The litmus test reflecting the status of relationships within one's school must be all-inclusive, the definition of No Child Left Behind we embrace. As we consider this question, our litmus test would consist of scheduling a faculty meeting attended by all teachers. They would come into a room where the walls were covered with chart paper. On each piece of chart paper would be the names of every student in the building with space left between the names. These names could be arranged in any manner that would facilitate the ability to locate the names of students easily from alphabetical order to grade level or even individual teacher rosters. Staff members would then be asked to find students on the list they knew and list two significant facts about who that child is without any discussion or talk among themselves. These significant facts could **not** include facts about academic performance or behavior at school. They should focus on knowing who the child is (their interests, gifts, obstacles, siblings, home life, etc). Would there be some students in your school with nothing under their names? What would you predict to be the outcome at your school? More importantly, how might you use the findings? Whether it is at the school level or the classroom level, the goal must be to know our students. Developing relationships must be intentional and with the same fervor as efforts geared toward assessment or even monitoring attendance.

We once read that teachers need to shut out everything else and focus on two things: what they teach and how they teach it. Immediately, we were saddened because the human element had been left out of this advice for teachers. When are we going to intentionally and systematically address the "who"? Who do we teach? This book has sought to outline not only relationships around a moral imperative and recovery, but also the importance of relationships and how they connect to curriculum, instruction, and assessment. High stakes accountability is alive and well. Teachers are continually barraged with countless expectations and priorities. There is extensive research to support an intentional focus on connections in schools.

Showing how relationships with students can correlate with curriculum, instruction, and assessment was necessary before some would believe relationships were "worthy" of planned, concentrated efforts of entire school faculty and staff. However, relationships around a moral imperative should be the genesis of school improvement efforts. It is through this dimension that students establish a sense of belonging, a need that exists for every student. Knowing those we teach is critical to our success as educators. To ignore them is to ignore the very essence of teaching and learning. So many assumptions are made about students and the level of their involvement in the educational process. We are often unaware and relegate coping with seemingly insurmountable obstacles as "not caring". There are even those within our profession who suggest students won't achieve because of their socioeconomic status or their home situations. Sadly, these educators have no idea of what those circumstances or obstacles are and exert little effort beyond finding excuses for poor performance. It's easy to blame the students. It takes courage to take ownership for all of our students.

From Black and White Snapshots to Color:

A country music artist, Jamey Johnson, sings the song, *In Color*. The song tells a story while a series of black and white photographs are being viewed. The breadth of experiences in the song is over the course of a lifetime. Examples of the lyrics include reminiscing about being involved in a war, as well as other significant events in the person's life.

> If it looks like we were scared to death like a couple of kids trying to save each other, *you should have seen it in color*….A picture's worth a thousand words but you can't see what those shades of gray cover, *you should have seen it in color…*

The lyrics are thought provoking, especially in the context of relationships and knowing our students. Seeing something and experiencing it are two different things. As educators, we see a black and white snapshot of our students at school every day. We only see the most obvious. We can't see all the shades of gray, nor do we truly know what it is like to be those students. We don't see their aspirations, self-perceptions, resources, support networks, interests, problems, obstacles, or family structures. We don't know the hunger pangs in the pit of their stomachs, the worry of when their next meal will be, or their attempts to remain warm on cold, snowy evenings. We don't know the fear of returning home because of abuse. We don't know the apprehension of returning to an unknown situation due to drugs, chronic or terminal illness. We can't even imagine the loneliness and self-doubt creeping into the lives of students who return home where a parent has left or is imprisoned, wondering what will happen, or why mom or dad left me. We don't know the self-defeat that becomes a constant companion when students are unable to read and do homework like their classmates. We don't know the sadness of coming to school where a student doesn't have any friends, or no one ever talks or treats them like a somebody. We don't see them *in color*. Reaching and teaching students means knowing them and often we don't even have a clue. All students, regardless of their situation, need to be acknowledged and need someone to believe in them. Students need teachers and schools to see them *in color*!

Chapter 8

Making it Happen:
Ideas To Think About

If a child is to keep alive his inborn sense of wonder, he needs the companionship of at least one adult who can share it, rediscovering with him the joy, excitement, and the mystery of the world we live in.

-Rachel Carson

Making It Happen

Education is perceived to be a caring profession, a helping profession. The reciprocity that occurs in a helping relationship is difficult to convey in words. John Maxwell often references the fact helping others is important to the giver and receiver, noting studies exist which suggest the higher one's level of helpfulness to others, the greater well-being one will experience. This statement illustrates what happens in healthy cultures where schools are focused on meeting the needs of students. However, this is not indicative of every school. Many schools are adult-centered and decisions sometimes occur in the absence of a discussion about how it will impact instruction and student success. In those schools and in some classrooms, a thinking shift must occur. Schools need to be staffed by well-trained and caring adults. However, schools must also re-examine their practices in light of the question, "Who's the first customer?" A commitment to student-centered schools is not as easy as it sounds because it necessitates that, in some situations, one will have to weigh the wishes of the adults against the needs of the students. However, we believe at the heart of good teaching is the heart of an adult who chose teaching as a profession because they wanted to make a difference. As schools, we must keep that mission in mind and constantly recalibrate our efforts in relation to the question posed by Martin Luther King, Jr. His statement is one that offers the opportunity to ruminate about our professional efforts. "Life's most persistent and urgent question is: What are you doing for others?" As schools, we must continually frame our discussions and actions around, what are we doing for students? How are we helping them be successful socially, emotionally, and academically?

A teacher's greatest reward is the feeling that occurs when students meet success. Knowing the views and opinions of students must serve as the impetus for transforming words into practice. What can schools and staff do to demonstrate relationships are the foundational element in creating a positive school culture focusing on the success of each student? Kudos and credit must be shared with great teachers whose creativity and ideas enable schools to embrace practices that focus on relationships around a moral imperative – it's the right thing to do. In addition to the twenty-nine ideas shared by students in the preceding chapters, there are multiple ways teachers convey to students this is a student-friendly classroom characterized by high expectations with everyone working together to realize success. The following list of ideas from practitioners demonstrates how effective teachers make it happen!

Eighty Ideas for Making It Happen!

1. Make a personal face-to-face contact with parents before the start of the school year. Make a visit to the home. Remember, you never get a second chance to make a first impression and it is difficult to change a first impression.
   - Conversation: Listen to find the gifts or talents of each student. Look for barriers to learning. Find out about the student's interests.
   - Take a digital camera on the home visit. Take a picture of the student and/or student and family. Picture can be used in variety of ways:
     - Student must find their picture and seat on the first day of school.
     - Create display with picture and future career choice.
   - Students are provided a bag or sack during the home visit. Each student will bring two items to school inside the bag that will represent something about himself or herself. One primary teacher gives two rules for this activity, the most important one being: "The items cannot be alive or used to be alive." The teacher also has a bag.

2. Create a business card magnet with your phone number and tell parents to call if they have a concern or in case there is an emergency. Ask for this same information including email address, if appropriate, from the parent. There is a good chance this magnet will be on every rcfrigerator.

3. Make a personal phone call after the first week of school to parents.
   - How was your child's first week of school?
   - Do you have any concerns? Are there any questions that need to be answered?
   - Invite parents to visit the classroom.

- Talk with a smile in your voice. (Remember the research on communicating by phone: 82% of communication on the phone has to do with tone of voice while only 18% is the words we use).

4. Send home handwritten positive notes or postcards throughout the year. Find something positive to say. Administrators often are willing to provide pre-paid postcards. You could also send a personal thank you card to each parent at the end of the year bragging on the positive qualities of their child. These cards can be sent at the end of the year. What parent would not love receiving a note about their child similar to the following?

Dear Mary,

   WOW! You have one **terrific** son. ***Brad*** is reading above grade level and has made so much progress this year. He is well respected by his classmates. ***Brad*** can make a friend in almost any situation and his confidence is always evident. He has a mischievous streak that keeps it interesting for the person working with him, but that doesn't keep one from appreciating the special young man he is. Keep him reading and connected to academic pursuits. Give **Mr. Winning Personality** a pat on the back. He is a keeper!

Dear Mr. and Mrs. Thompson

   Even though ***Taylor*** is quiet, you can be sure he is observing things and knows what is going on in class. I am really proud ***of Taylor***. He has made tremendous progress in reading and math. ***Taylor*** has a great attitude toward school and learning. He is always ready to start the day and accomplish goals he sets for himself. ***Taylor*** is a fine young man who will always do the right thing. That is a wonderful characteristic in anyone. Thank you for sharing your **very special son** with me this year. He is truly **AWESOME!**

                                                            Mrs. G.

Dear Ann and Michael,

   Did they break the mold when Claire was born? The answer is: *Absolutely!* I don't have enough adjectives to describe how special Claire is as a student and as a person. My day begins the same every day - a greeting from Claire with outstretched arms and a great big hug. What will I do next year? She is such a ray of sunshine in the lives of everyone she encounters. You are terrific parents and I am confident that Claire will be successful in whatever endeavor or field she chooses. She is an outstanding communicator and wins the title of "drama queen." Love her a little for me every day because she is **truly remarkable!**

                                                            Mrs. G.

5. Find a way to help parents deal with bureaucracy and paperwork. Have a way to help parents complete the forms at the beginning of the year. Ask questions to determine if a parent who has multiple children in the school system is required to fill out the same forms. Is there some way that a parent can complete only one form for all students. A second option that our district is utilizing is to copy a print-off of the information from previous year. If all the information is the same, the parent simply signs the form.

6. When students leave school at the end of the day and go home, one of the questions that is asked is, "What did you do at school today?" To avoid the response every educator scowls at, "Nothing!" help students be more prepared to give an appropriate response. Create a fun game to review the activities of the day and week so students will have specific responses to the inquiry, "What did you learn at school today?" One elementary teacher has students form a circle at the end of the day and the students throw a beach ball to each other to review what was learned that day. The teacher also discusses that sharing the response, "nothing" with parents is not acceptable. Adapt the idea for a middle school team or a high school homeroom or closure at the end of a lesson.

7. Provide daily or weekly progress reports to parents. Many schools have student agendas that can be utilized. Be consistent with methods.
   - Keep a folder for each student's work which can be sent home, signed, and returned to school.
   - Keep a log in your classroom students sign when they fail to do their work.
   - Make a commitment to accurate and timely recording of grades, especially if parents can access their child's grade electronically on a regular basis.

8. Create color-coded pre-excuse letters and bus notes. Then, all parents have to do is to fill in their child's name, sign, and date. Parents are often nervous and struggle with saying the right thing and some are fearful of making spelling mistakes and being ridiculed.

Straub Elementary	**Straub Elementary**
My child, _____ _____ was absent on _____ because _____. *Parent signature:* _____ *Date:* _____ (Blue paper)	My child, _____ will be riding bus # _____ on _____ *(date)* to _____. (*Name & Address of Destination [Example: Betty William's house @ 123 Main Street, Maysville]*) I can be reached at _____ if you have any questions. *Parent signature:* _____ *Date:* _____ *(Red paper)*

Straub Elementary	Straub Elementary
My child, _____ will be picked up at school on _____ by *(Date)* _____. I can be reached at _____ if you have any questions. *Parent signature:* _____ *Date:* _____ *(Yellow paper)*	My child, _____ had an upsetting event that happened. He/she may have a difficult time at school today. I just wanted you to know that: _____ *(brief statement of what happened; i.e. death, illness, injur {for example: grandfather died, pet died; mother hospitalized, etc)* and if you have questions or concerns, I can be reached at _____. ***Parent signature:*** _____ ***Date:*** _____ *(Green paper)*

9. Create a brochure about yourself. Include items such as your degree, your hobbies and interests, and a little about your family. Share information about your classroom, your expectations, and what students will be learning. You can even provide ways to contact you. Give to parents during your first meeting with them.

10. Create opportunities to invite parents, guardians, or grandparents into the classroom. Classroom plays, performances, and even guest speakers are examples of ways to open the classroom to important partners in students' success. Find a way to learn about the talents of parents and utilize them when appropriate.

11. Have an end of the year Showcase of Excellence. During this, all students would have "exhibits" of some of their best work they created or did throughout the year along with descriptions of the content or example of scoring guide. If possible, keep some of this best work for mental models for future students.

12. Consider a get-together before the first day of school as an opportunity for classmates, parents, and teachers to get to know each other. Some teachers have hosted swim parties, picnics, or pizza parties at safe and appropriate locations. Others have sponsored an evening at school with grilled hot dogs or ice cream sundaes as a way to introduce students and parents to a new classroom.

13. Think about organizing a potluck or get together at the end of the year. Take pictures throughout the year and design a power point with music recapturing special moments and events throughout the year. Give each parent a disk copy.

14. Create a scrapbook for each child. Involve the students and work on them periodically throughout the year with special attention given to memorable events in the student's life. It could contain pictures, art work, writings, samples of student work, or mementos from special experiences throughout the year. Gives to parents at the end of the year.

15. Invite parents to a parent teacher conference with a personal phone call. Express a genuine interest and extend the invitation in a welcoming manner. Treat all parents as if they might be your next school board member. When parents attend the conference, truly listen to their concerns. Sit around a table as opposed to sitting behind a desk. If it is a parent teacher night at school, try to schedule conferences. Some teachers even provide refreshments in a waiting area. If the designated time frame for conference elapses and there are still parents waiting, take the time to talk with each. It is a negative reflection on the teacher and the school when the teacher refuses to conference with parents because the scheduled conference time has expired.

16. Give parents a monthly newsletter with a calendar of events. Utilize the USA Today philosophy by incorporating several pictures and bulleting items of interest. Minimize the amount of verbiage. If possible, develop a class e-mail distribution list for parents and send via e-mail. Send a hard copy if e-mail is not an option.

17. Create a classroom webpage. Once the webpage is created, make a commitment to keeping it updated. Parents express frustration when they consult web pages on a regular basis for homework assignments or classroom updates and the web page is two or three weeks behind schedule.

18. Remain updated with factual information about the district and the school. Be a positive public relations agent for your school and district. Know what makes your school or district a great place for students and education. Familiarize yourself with assessment results, extracurricular opportunities, teacher and student ratio, additional programming, and available technology. Remember, when you speak negatively about the place that employs you, you are speaking negatively about yourself.

19. As a teacher, you are a leader in your school and in your classroom. Be proactive and think about expectations and the conduct of other adults in the classroom such as volunteers and instructional assistants. Communicate this to respective individuals. Ensure your classroom is a place where all adults focus on helping all children be successful and not a forum for adult issues and the internal politics of the school. Check with building leadership to determine if school wide expectations exist or training is provided. For example, it would be imperative to train anyone assisting in the classroom in confidentiality.

20. Professionally frame your teaching credentials and diplomas. Hang them in the classroom. These are a reflection of your professional qualifications and training. Be proud of these. Not only do they represent milestones in your life, they are valuable as visual reminders to students about their goals.

21. Share success stories. It is human nature to find problems and negative aspects to discuss. Think about the successes students are experiencing in your classroom and share these with your friends on a regular basis. These anecdotes will be repeated. Good customer service companies find ways to get the word out!

22. Everyone loves a compliment. Don't forget to share your appreciation for assistance face-to-face, as well as with other people. This even includes your administrators. Comments about others always usually find their way to the doorsteps of the person you are discussing. It is almost impossible to give something positive without getting something back in return. Words can be used as tools or weapons. Make your words tools for building and not weapons of destruction.

23. Become a member and attend the meetings of your school's parent and teacher organization. Parents love to see you there.

24. Speak to students and parents whenever you see them. As teachers, know the names and use them. Have a seating chart and take a digital picture on the first day. Call students by name on the second day of school. Building administrators should work to learn as many of the names of students and parents as possible.

25. Keep the school and the classrooms neat and attractive. Paint your walls with good examples of *student* work. Keep in mind the following:
    - Rooms should be free of clutter
        - Word walls and content posters should be posted when introduced and utilized in the course of the lesson. They should not be placed on the wall at the beginning of the year. In many high-performing schools, students create the charts which are then placed on the walls with reminders of key ideas.
        - Place content descriptors with displays of student work so that others know the context and the learning target of the displayed work.
        - Change displays of student work on a regular basis.
        - Personalize the displays, when appropriate. Some teachers have display mats with student names and pictures and then a space to display their work. One teacher reported that when she placed the faces of students on racing cars on a track with reading goals, several students worked harder and read more.
    - Desks need to be clean and free of marks
        - Involve the students in keeping desks clean.
        - Teach responsibility for your desk, the floor around you, your messes and the room. (Teach respect for the custodian).
        - Teach this as part of a classroom routine or procedure.
    - No bad smells (Students discuss how they remember classrooms with pleasant scents)
    - No graffiti
    - Vents are clean
    - No dead bugs in lights

26. Create a refrigerator door in your classroom or outside your classroom to display student work or positive notes. Remember, parents place their children's work on the refrigerator. Be a teacher who is proud of students' work and accomplishments!

27. Dress as a professional. While there will be times when other attire may be appropriate for classroom or school activities, it is important that we remember we are professionals and should dress the part. Jeans and school spirit gear have their place, but are not part of the daily dress code for educators.

28. Keep confidential information confidential. If there is a classroom management or school wide discipline system where the names of students are placed on charts or boards, use a numbering system instead of names of students.

29. Own the parent's question or problem. Listen to the concern and work with the parent to try to resolve the issue instead of passing it off or playing the blame game.

30. Encourage students and families to set aside 20-30 minutes each evening for a family Read-a-Thon. Help students and families develop a love for reading.

31. Attend performances or events of students outside the regular school day. These could include events such as church performances, sporting events, musicals, cattle shows, beauty pageants, birthday parties, academic team meets, and other similar activities. Make sure students see you there and they know you are there to support them. If you do not talk to the student at the event, make sure you say something informally about it the next school day.

32. Send invitations to grandparents for Grandparent's Day. Have them collaborate with their grandchild to complete a class activity. Take pictures of grandparents interacting with students. Mail pictures to them with a note thanking them for spending time with your class.

33. Return all phone calls and e-mails within twenty-four hours. If you are going to be out for a few days, leave an out of the office e-mail message that informs everyone you are currently not available to respond to their inquiry.

34. Visit students who are hospitalized. Send cards with handwritten notes from other students. Let students know they are missed, you are concerned about their well-being, and you will work with them to help with missed work.

35. ALWAYS remain with a student or students who are injured, have missed a bus, or are late being picked up by parents. This applies to all students, whether they are kindergarten or seniors ready to graduate.

36. Inform the school office if you have changed the location of your class. The office needs to know where to find you or your students at all times. Some teachers also use a locator

on their door or in the hallway with an arrow showing where they are if someone should come to the classroom and find it empty (i.e. gym, lunchroom, outside, library, etc). The last student out of the door places the arrow on where the class will be or hangs it on the door handle.

37. After obtaining approval for a field trip or field experience, be sure to think about the following:
    - Make proper notifications to the bus garage and to the food service director. (Each of these departments may need to make adjustments to schedules or number of lunches served based on your information. The nutrition staff also needs to be aware in advance if sack lunches are to be packed for students who are scheduled to go on the field trip. Make sure you always have them make one or two extra lunches).
    - If some parents plan on driving separately and accompanying the class, provide them with a destination map.
    - Leave a copy of the itinerary and class phone tree with the office. Leave your cell phone number with the office.
    - When planning a trip, plan for the worst case scenario (inclement weather, bus problems). Have a plan prepared should the situation arise. Many teachers use phone trees to notify parents if delays occur.
    - If the trip is cancelled, let everyone know about cancellation (principal, bus garage, food service, parents).

38. Know that your immediate supervisor needs to be aware of problems or potential problems in advance. No one likes to be caught off-guard or unaware of a situation that can escalate without having the background knowledge only you can provide.

39. Do not bring your personal problems into the classroom. This is the same expectation we have when services are rendered from other professionals (i.e. doctors, dentists, bankers, service occupations) and we should not expose our "customers" to our personal problems. It is appropriate for students to have a general knowledge relating to your absence or need to take a phone call. However, these should be general comments such as an illness. Class time is not the time for engaging in detailed discussions about one's personal problems.

40. Remember, you are in control of your attitude, no matter what happens in school or happens to you personally. No one is responsible for your individual morale other than yourself.

41. Try to have the solution to problems before you talk with the principal or administrator. For example, "I have an emergency and need to leave school ten minutes early. Mrs. Smith said she would cover my class." When you continually share problems with the office and do not have any solutions, most administrators will view this behavior as whining.

42. Find additional resources to address the needs of students in your classroom. There may be students who are hungry, students with lice, students who need glasses or any wide variety of issues that are barriers to learning. View these as opportunities and enlist the assistance of community agencies or volunteers in addressing these needs in ways that are not demeaning to students. Knowing and understanding Abraham Maslow's Hierarchy of Needs alludes to the importance of such acts.

43. Capitalize on the customer service practice to under-promise and over-deliver, when appropriate. For example, if scoring an exam, share with students you will have it completed in two days. However, give them back the next day. This is a mindset. Think about going to a restaurant. They share it will be a twenty minute wait, but you are seated within ten minutes. How does it make you feel? However, if you are told twenty minutes and it takes thirty minutes, you are upset.

44. Walk visitors to their destination, when possible. If you have volunteers or students who work in the office, teach them how to interact with guests and how to walk the guests to their destination.

45. Never spread gossip (even if you know it to be true) about students, parents, other teachers, or administrators. True professionals never make derogatory remarks about others in the community. How many conversations can you recall where doctors made disparaging remarks about other doctors or even their patients?

46. Avoid negative colleagues. You can rest assured the negativity they are expressing about others will eventually target you. Negative individuals seek to recruit others to their causes. Other teachers refuse to get involved because they want to focus on their students Never lose sight of the realization students are the reasons we have jobs. They, in effect, sign our paychecks. Therefore, we need to remain focused on students and not negative situations.

47. Eat with the students at least once a week. Think about rewarding the class by allowing them to come back and eat in the classroom. Eating with students fosters relationship-building.

48. The school should have a well-designed program for accommodating new students. However, as a teacher you should develop some classroom welcoming procedures and routines for new students (regardless of how you truly feel). Be creative.
    - Could the class give a standing ovation when a new student enters the classroom?
    - Could you take the time to have a get-to know-you lunch with the new student and another classmate?
    - Make sure the new student has someone to eat lunch with on their first few days at a new school.
    - Follow-up with the parent or guardian after the first day and do a second follow-up after one or two weeks. Help answer any concerns or questions.

49. Impress your administration by handling almost all problems within your own classroom. Avoid sending students to the office for petty issues such as no pencil or paper brought to class. In fact, have extra pencils and extra paper in your classroom. If you are unsure how to handle a situation, ask for advice from a colleague or even the building administrator. This shows you are attempting to handle your own problems. Remember, no one has all the answers.

50. Train students on classroom routines so they know what to do when any guest enters the classroom or there is a call. Teach how to answer the phone, how to greet a guest, (if appropriate), voice level, and your expectations when a guest enters the classroom. Good classroom management is impressive to everyone.

51. Train a student to be an ambassador for substitute teachers. This ambassador will answer the door when the teacher is absent and explain to the visitor that the regular teacher is absent and share what the class is currently studying or doing.

52. Have your class adopt a section of the school either inside or outside and keep their section clean. They could pick up trash, water plants, and try to leave the area better than they found it.

53. Evaluate your school supply list in terms of needs and expense. Let parents know early in the summer what they need to purchase. When evaluating the school supply list, think about the following:
    - Do not use name brands.
    - Make sure products are easily available.
    - Ask for donations instead if demanding supplies. Create an angel tree for supplies.
    - Inform parents about school supply donation programs.

    An alternative to parents purchasing supplies is for the teacher or school to collect a fee from each parent and then place an order for each student that is sent directly to you. (Check on your school's protocol concerning ordering materials).

54. Ask the students not to exchange Christmas gifts or to bring you gifts. Instead, do a class fundraiser and buy gifts for needy child or family. Visit a local food pantry, identify needs, shop as a class, and then take to food pantry.

55. Take a picture of your class. Keep the picture and send to students when they graduate from high school. Inquire if newspaper will print picture congratulating students on their successful completion of school and wishing them well in their post-secondary pursuits.

56. Have students write down one positive thing about each student in the classroom. Give to each student at the end of the year. (Remember the statistic that 80% of students have a positive self-perception when they enter school. By the end of 5th grade, it drops to 20%).

57. Praise students or send congratulatory notes home when students improve or achieve a goal. As E.M. Cioran reminds us: "If each of us were to confess his most secret desire, the one that inspires all his plans, all his actions, he would say, I want to be praised."

58. Have a good supply of books and games that represent various cultures of students within the classroom. Cultivate a love for reading by having books with characters who reflect the culture of students in the classroom. Invite guest speakers who represent various cultures.

59. Develop a good relationship with the newspaper and radio. Send information to be shared on a regular basis. Have the editor on your class distribution e-mail list. Create a form that can be faxed directly to the newspaper.

60. Send a summer postcard introducing yourself and welcoming students to your class.

61. Purchase small gifts for appreciation to have on hand for events such as secretary's day, bus driver appreciation, boss's day, nutrition services appreciation day, or school board recognition. Gifts could include handwritten notes or drawings from students. Show appreciation for classified workers and volunteers throughout the year.

62. Start and end every parent meeting and conversation with a positive comment about the child.

63. Be a mentor to all new teachers or any teacher that needs help. Zig Ziglar maintains that "You can get everything in life you want if you will just help enough other people get what they want." John Maxwell shares in his writings and speeches that helping others grow is the highest form of leadership.

64. Call home after a student misses two days of class in a row. Share that you miss the student and look forward to their return. Use the phone in the classroom and have class share in unison, "We miss you!" If the parent or child is worried about the work, tell parents how the student can make up the work and how to access materials.

65. Convey to students this class operates and functions as a family. Everyone has responsibilities for keeping classroom clean, for encouraging and helping each other, and for doing their best. Students need safe and secure learning environments. Students also need desks and spaces that belong to them as part of this secure learning environment.

66. Discipline students individually. Do not subject students to group punishment. We do not like that philosophy as adults or as educators and neither do students.

67. Have a first aid kit readily available when students are injured on playground. If a student is injured or has a scrape or cut, communicate to the parents or guardians so they know what happened.

68. Give each student a hug or high five before they enter the classroom. If that is not your personality, at least greet each student as they enter.

69. Interact in a positive manner with students at recess, during a break, or during informal moments.

70. Have the expectation and teach classroom routines related to expected behavior when others are speaking. Is there an expectation of "zero voice" when announcements are being made or when the principal calls the room?

71. Never embarrass students in front of the class. No one deserves to be embarrassed or humiliated in front of their peers. Even though most of us can recall a story when this occurred in our lives, it is one of the most damaging and destructive practices that can occur in classrooms. Students' number one fear is being humiliated in front of their peers.

72. Teach with the brain in mind. Remember the brain retains information better when material is presented using the CUE strategy. CUE stands for creative, useful, or emotional.

73. Notice the students. Make positive comments about a new hair cut, new clothes, new car, shoes and other similar experiences. Think about the first day of school or picture day. Students' faces light up with big smiles when someone makes a comment about how good they look. Don't wait for special days to acknowledge students. Every student has an invisible sign around their neck that says, "Notice me. Acknowledge ways I am special!"

74. Observe student body language and note any students with the demeanor, "I'm having a bad day!" Some schools are adept at this and observe students as soon as they enter the building at the beginning of the school day. This enables them to be proactive and address any issues that might impact the school day.

75. Give students second chances and the opportunity to learn from their mistakes.

76. Address rumors or criticism. Share information with the appropriate stakeholder so that correct information can be communicated.

77. Use songs and music to improve instruction. Use music appropriately in the classroom. At the primary level, many teachers use music for transition or as part of their classroom routines. Music can be very effective in teaching routines. In classrooms with older students, teachers use music for calming effects or play music in the background while students are working.

78. Be intentional about having informal conversations with students. A high percentage of students never have a conversation with an adult.

79. Think about how to bring the outdoors inside the classroom. Students seem to have a natural connection to appropriate pets in the class. (Make sure you arrange for the care of plants or animals over extended breaks).

80. Attend the graduation ceremony, regardless of the grade level you teach. One of the aspirations of schools is to have all students graduate from high school. Graduation is a ceremony attesting to the collective effort of all throughout a student's educational career.

Customer service is a mindset. It is a commitment to see an issue from the customer's perspective. As educators, the working environment is rich with opportunities to incorporate customer service ideas into our interactions and communication with students and other stakeholders. Students can share what makes school meaningful for them. There are multiple ideas, such as the eighty listed above from creative and caring educators, which make schools a great place to learn. Schools characterized by fractured relationships are not good places to be. For us, the question of school improvement and what is most important in schools begins with reflecting on the interactions between teachers and students as well as the interactions among other stakeholders in the educational process. Since students are the first customers, we must constantly scrutinize our actions and begin intentional and systematic efforts. Hopefully, readers will have a greater appreciation for the power of relationships and make a commitment to incorporating some of the ideas from the research voice and from the student voice.

Self-Assessment Tools

The opportunity to reflect was provided at the end of each chapter. You were asked to think about your experiences as a student and then as an educator. Hopefully, you spent some time thinking about relationships around each of the dimensions: Relationships Around a Moral Imperative, Relationships Around the Curriculum, Relationships Around Assessment, and

Relationships Around Recovery. Questionnaires are provided in the following pages asking you to think about where you are in relation to the concepts from the student voice, as well as from the research voice. Use these as avenues for determining what you are willing to commit to and deciding on next steps for you or your school.

One final note, the reflections and self assessment opportunities presented are not meant to point fingers at anyone. We are aware of the many demands existing in classrooms and schools. However, it was our goal for you to conceptualize the myriad of ways you influence and make an impact on students through your relationships with them. Know you make a difference. Be assured an intentional focus on relationship building among all stakeholders is a wise investment of time and effort. There are many ways to begin and there is not a blueprint which will work for all teachers or all schools. The most important thing is just to begin and take those initial steps. Learn who your students are. Work to ensure interactions between teachers and students are positive ones. Think about what you want for your own child! Be committed and know the journey you or your school embarks on around relationships is one of the most important expeditions that will lead to new discoveries about students and learning.

Student Voice Self Assessment

Relationships Around a Moral Imperative

When I reflect on how I interact with students:

	All the Time	*Some of the Time*	*Seldom*	*Future Goal for Me*
1. I know each of my students personally. I know their interests and what they enjoy doing.				
2. I share appropriate information about myself with students so they know who I am as a person.				
3. I smile at my students throughout the day.				
4. I quickly learn my students' names and use them throughout the day.				
5. I speak to my students throughout the day and when I see them in public. I make it a point to greet each one and to tell them good-bye.				
6. I tease or joke in a fun and appropriate way with my students during informal situations.				
7. I visit my students at their homes before school begins.				
8. I personally call or visit when one of my students or their family members are ill to check and see how they are doing.				
9. I share information about school events with students and encourage each student to participate in extracurriculars based on his/her interests.				
10. I attend important events or activities of my students such as games, recitals, or plays.				
11. I establish rules and expectations that are applicable to everyone in the classroom, including myself.				
12. I make it a point to be fair to all students in my classroom and do not show favoritism in words or actions to any one student.				
13. I am consistent in my interactions and expectations with each student in the classroom.				
14. I make it a priority to do something special (such as cook) or share my talent or interests with my students during the year.				
15. I make sure I treat students with respect before, during, and after school in my conversations with colleagues and others.				

Relationships Around Curriculum

When I reflect on how I plan curricular experiences for students:

	All the Time	Some of the Time	Seldom	Future Goal for Me
16. I share why students need to do things.				
17. I discuss the relevance of the content and how students can apply the information they are learning in real-world situations.				
18. I embed experiences that enable students to use their problem solving and thinking skills around issues that will impact others or their future.				

Relationships Around Instruction

When I reflect on my instruction,

	All the Time	Some of the Time	Seldom	Future Goal for Me
19. I use effective practices such as hands-on activities that focus on student engagement. I remain current with best practices and the latest research.				
20. I use technology when presenting the content. I also find ways for students to use their own technology when appropriate.				
21. I give meaningful work to students that promote understanding, as well as application and analysis of ideas. I do not assign busy work such as word searches or overuse worksheets.				
22. I am energetic and enthusiastic about my content and students know I enjoy my job.				
23. I provide help or additional assistance to students on my own time (afterschool, early mornings, lunch, planning).				
24. I am in control of the class and have good classroom management skills. I ensure students have an appropriate environment for learning				

Relationships Around Assessment

When I reflect on assessments in my classroom,

	All the Time	*Some of the Time*	*Seldom*	*Future Goal for Me*
25. I provide feedback to my students that helps them know how to improve (specific) and feedback that is provided in a timely manner.				
26. I value the work and effort of my students. I am careful never to demean students or their work.				
27. I convey to all students my belief in their ability to improve. I try to find ways that enable students to experience success.				

Relationships Around Recovery

When I reflect on mistakes that occur at school,

	All the Time	*Some of the Time*	*Seldom*	*Future Goal for Me*
28. I admit to students when I mess up or make a mistake.				
29. I take up for students if they are being mistreated. I will work to make sure a situation is addressed if a student has been treated unfairly, even among my colleagues.				

Research Voice Self-Assessment

Relationships Around a Moral Imperative
When I reflect on how I interact with students:

	All the Time	Some of the Time	Seldom	Future Goal for Me
I know my students, their interests, and their situations. I see my students as individuals.				
I have high expectations for all my students, working with each to establish goals. My students know I believe in them and will work to help them be successful.				
I create an atmosphere of mutual trust and respect. I work to preserve the dignity of each learner.				
I show students I care about them based on my words and actions. I check on students and am genuine.				
I encourage my students to become involved in school activities based on their needs and interests.				
I work to personalize the learning environment and promote a focus on "our" classroom. I provide positive recognition of student success and progress.				

Relationships Around Curriculum
When I reflect on how I plan curricular experiences for students:

	All the Time	Some of the Time	Seldom	Future Goal for Me
I plan lessons that inform students how they will be able to apply what they are learning. I focus on why the content is meaningful or interesting.				
I link student interests to curricular concepts when developing lessons or units of study.				
I focus on the background knowledge students bring to a learning task. I deliberately plan ways I can build or activate student background knowledge related to the content being studied.				
I write and communicate clear learning targets that are written in student-friendly language for each lesson.				
I look for opportunities for interdisciplinary lessons or connections with the content I am teaching. I collaboratively plan and integrate curricular ideas with other teachers.				
I display student work and look for opportunities to showcase student work throughout the school.				

194

Relationships Around Instruction
When I reflect on my instruction,

	All the Time	Some of the Time	Seldom	Future Goal for Me
I utilize a variety of research based practices during instruction, focusing on selection of appropriate strategies for specific outcomes.				
I incorporate multiple opportunities for students to actively learn and make sense of their learning.				
I find ways to emotionally engage students in the lesson when appropriate.				
I plan for and ask higher level questions during lessons that require critical or creative thinking.				
I focus on incorporating student choice in classroom activities or assignments.				
I convey to my students that I am interested in their learning and their success. I create an environment where it is acceptable to make mistakes and learn from them.				
I provide students with additional support or individual help when it is needed.				

Relationships Around Assessment
When I reflect on assessments in my classroom,

	All the Time	Some of the Time	Seldom	Future Goal for Me
I carefully plan the first assessment of the year so that all students will be successful.				
I involve my students in setting, monitoring and assessing goals for learning.				
I incorporate frequent formative assessments in my classroom and use the results to inform instruction.				
I provide descriptive feedback to students. My feedback enables them to know how their work compares to a standard and gives them specifics on how to improve.				
I utilize student self-assessment and reflection on a routine basis.				
I utilize assessment results to provide corrective instruction if students have not learned the content. I use results for enrichment or differentiated experiences if students demonstrate mastery.				

Relationships Around Recovery

When I reflect on mistakes that occur at school,

	All the Time	Some of the Time	Seldom	Future Goal for Me
I apologize quickly (within 24 hours) when I make a mistake.				
I am sincere and empathetic when I offer an apology. I realize it is about the other person, not me.				
I communicate to the offended party that the mistake will not be repeated.				
My apology equals the offense. If I made the mistake in public, I apologize in public.				
I ask the injured party if the situation or issue has been resolved to their satisfaction.				
When possible, I try to add a personal touch to my apologies through a follow-up note or small gift.				

References

Akey, T. M. (2006, January). *School context, student attitudes and behavior, and academic achievement: An exploratory analysis.* New York: MDRC. Retrieved September 12, 2009 from http://www.mdrc.org/publications/419/full.pdf

Ancess, J. (2008, May). Small alone is not enough. How can educators recover the purposes of small schools? *Educational Leadership*, 48-53

Barnerias, C. (2007, June 12). *7 Powerful tips on how to say sorry gracefully.* Retrieved November 19, 2009 from http://ezinearticles.com/?7-Powerful-Tips-on-How-to-Say-Sorry-Gracefully&id=602779

Barr, R. & Parrett, W. (2008). *Saving our students saving our schools 50 proven strategies for helping underachieving students and improving schools.* Thousand Oaks, CA: Corwin Press.

Barr, R. & Parrett, W. (2007). *The kids left behind catching up the underachieving children of poverty.* Bloomington, IN: Solution Tree.

Beilick, S. (2008, December). 1.5 million homeschooled students in the United States in 2007. *National Center for Education Statistic Issue Brief.* Washington, D.C.: United States Department of Education.

Benard, B. (2003). Turnaround teachers and schools. In B. Williams (Ed.). *Closing the achievement gap a vision for changing beliefs and practices* (pp.115-137). Alexandria, VA: Association for Supervision and Curriculum Development.

Black, P., Harrison, C., Lee, C., Marshall, B., & Wilian, D. (2003). *Assessment for learning. Putting it into practice.* New York, NY: Open University Press.

Blanchard, K. & McBride, M. (2003). *The one minute apology, A powerful way to make things better.* New York: William Morrow.

Bondy, E. & Ross, D. (2008, September). The teacher as warm demander. *Educational Leadership*, 54-58.

Bowlby, J. (1989). *The making and breaking of affectional bonds.* New York, NY: Routledge.

Bridgeland, J., Dilulio, J., & Morison, K. (2006, March). *The silent epidemic perspectives of high school dropouts.* Washington, D.C.: Civic Enterprises in association with Peter D. Hart Research Associates.

Bronfenbrenner, U. (1991, Winter/Spring). What do families do? *Family Affairs*, 2-6.

Bronfenbrenner, U. (1994). Who cares for the children? In H. Nuba, M. Searson, & D. Sheiman (Eds.). *Resources for early childhood: A handbook* (pp. 113-129). New York: Garland

Brooks, R. (2002, April). *Violence prevention in our schools: Promoting a sense of belonging.* Retrieved November 20, 2009 from www.drrobertbrooks.com.

Carnegie, D. (1981). *How to win friends and influence people.* New York: Pocket Books.

Center for Comprehensive School Reform and Improvement. (2007, April). *Using positive student engagement to increase student achievement.* Washington, DC: Learning Center Associates, Retrieved December 1, 2009 from www.**center**forcsri.org/index.php?option=com_content&task...id...

Christensen, C., Johnson, C., & Horn, M. (2008). *Disrupting class: How disruptive innovation will change the way the world learns.* New York, NY: McGraw-Hill.

Christensen, L. (2008, September). Welcoming all languages. *Educational Leadership,* 59-62.

Clarke, S. (2005). *Formative assessment in action weaving the elements together.* London: Hodder Murray.

Cleveland, R. (n.d.). *Learning Styles* [PowerPoint Slides] Retrieved October 15, 2009 from www.moreheadstate.edu/files/colleges/education/.../learningstyles.pdf

Cockerell, L. (2008). *Creating magic 10 common sense leadership strategies from a life at disney.* New York: Broadway Business

Cornbleth, C. (n.d.). *School curriculum – Hidden curriculum.* Retrieved October 20, 2009 from http://education.stateuniversity.com/pages/1899/Curriculum-School-HIDDEN-CURRIC

Cottrell, D. (2007). *Monday morning choices: 12 powerful ways to go from everyday to extraordinary.* New York: Harper Collins.

Covey, S. (2003). *The seven habits of highly effective people.* New York: Fireside Publishing.

Cowan, D. (2008, January 31). We are hardwired to connect with others. *EzineArticles.* Retrieved February 8, 2008, from http://ezines.com/?We-Are-Hardwired-To-Connect-With-Others&id=960335

Curwood, J.S. (2009, August). Wired up: Tuned out. *Scholastic Administrator.* 52-55.

Darling-Hammond, L. & Friedlaender, D. (2008, May). Creating excellent and equitable schools. *Educational Leadership,* 14-21.

Davies, A. (2007). Involving students in the assessment process. In D. Reeves (Ed.), *Ahead of the curve. The power of assessment to transform teaching and learning* (pp. 31-57). Bloomington, IN: Solution Tree

.
Denove, C. & Powers, J.D. (2006). *Satisfaction: How every great company listens to the voice of the customer.* New York: Penguin Group

Dijulius, J.R. (2008). *What's the secret? To providing a world class customer service experience.* Hoboken, NJ: John Wiley & Sons, Inc.

Dufour, R., Dufour, R., Eaker, R. & Many, T. (2006). *Learning by doing: A handbook for professional learning communities at work.* Bloomington, IN: Solution Tree.

Dunsworth, M. & Billings, D. (2009*). The high performing school: Benchmarking the 10 indicators of effectiveness.* Bloomington, IN: Solution Tree.

Earthling Communication (2007, March 19). *How to apologize correctly: Part 3. Retrieved November 19, 2009 from* http://www,earthlingcommunication.com/blog/how-to-apologize-correctly-part-3.php

Engel, B. (2001). *The power of apology: Healing steps to transform all your relationships.* New York: John Wiley & Sons.

Feynman, R. (n.d.). *About 4 temperaments.* Retrieved July 2008 from http://keirsey.com/handler.aspx?s=keirsey&f=fourtemps&tab=5&c=feynman#

Fisher, D. & Frey, N. (2007). *Checking for understanding formative assessment techniques for your classroom.* Alexandria, VA: Association for Supervision and Curriculum Development.

Fuchs, L. & Fuchs, D. (1986). Effects of systematic formative evaluation: A meta-analysis. *Exceptional Children, 53(3),* 199-208.

Fullan, M. (2008). *The six secrets of change - What the best leaders do to help their organizations survive and thrive.* San Francisco, CA: Jossey-Bass

Futrell, M. H. & Gomez, J. (2008, May). How tracking creates a poverty of learning. *Educational Leadership*, 86-87.

Gilbert, R. & Robins, M. (1998). *Welcome to our world: Realities of high school students.* Thousand Oaks, CA: Corwin Press.

Guskey, T. (2008, August 20). *Grading and Reporting Student Learning.* Indianapolis, IN: HOPE Foundation Indianapolis Summit.

Guskey, T. (2007). Using assessments to improve teaching and learning. In D. Reeves (Ed.), *Ahead of the curve. The power of assessment to transform teaching and learning* (pp. 15-29). Bloomington, IN: Solution Tree

Haycock, K. (2003, May 20). *Testimony of Kati Haycock, president, Education Trust before the U.S. House of Representative committee on education and the workforce subcommittee on 21st century competitiveness* Retrieved January 7, 2010 from http://www.edtrust.org/dc/press-room/statement-testimony/testimony-of-kati-haycock-president-the-education-trust-before-the

Heller, R., Calderon, S., & Medrich, E. (2003). *Academic achievement in the middle grades: What does research tell us? A review of the literature.* Atlanta, GA: Southern Regional Education Board. Retrieved September 12, 2009, from http://www.sreb.org/programs/hstw/publications/pubs/02V47_AchievementReview.pdf

Hierck, T. (2009). Formative assessment, transformative relationships. In T. Guskey (Ed.), *The principal as assessment leader.* Bloomington, IN: Solution Tree.

Hill, C. (2009, January). Making connections. *American School Board Journal,* 18.

Jackson, R. (2009). *Never work harder than your students & other principles of great teaching.* Alexandria, VA: Association for Supervision and Curriculum Development

James, D. W. (ed) (1997). *Some things do make a difference for youth: A compendium of evaluations of youth programs and practices.* Washington, DC: American Youth Policy Forum.

Jensen, E. (2005). *Teaching with the brain in mind.* Alexandria, VA: Association for Supervision and Curriculum Development

Klem, A. & Connell, R. (2004, September). Relationships matter: Linking teacher support to student engagement and achievement. *Journal of School Health,* 262-273.

Kobrin, D. (2004). *In there with the kids crafting lessons that connect with the students.* Alexandria, VA: Association for Supervision and Curriculum Development

Kohn, A. (2006). *Beyond discipline from compliance to community.* Alexandria, VA: Association for Supervision and Curriculum Development.

Leaf, M. (1936), *The story of Ferdinand.* New York: Puffin Books.

Malouff, J. et al (2008). *Methods of motivational teaching.* Educational Resources Information Center (ED499496). Retrieved February 8, 2008 from http://www.eric.ed.gov/ERICWebPortal/Home.portal?_nfpb=true&ERICExtSearch_

Marzano, R. (2004). *Building background knowledge for academic achievement: Research on what works in schools.* Alexandria, VA: Association for Supervision and Curriculum Development

Marzano, R. (2007*).* Designing a comprehensive classroom assessment. In D. Reeves (Ed.), *Ahead of the curve. The power of assessment to transform teaching and learning* (pp. 103-125). Bloomington, IN: Solution Tree

Marzano, R. (2009). *Designing & teaching learning goals & objectives classroom strategies that work.* Bloomington, IN: Marzano Research Laboratory

Marzano, R. (2007*).* *The art and science of teaching: A comprehensive framework for effective instruction.* Alexandria, VA: Association for Supervision and Curriculum Development

Maxwell, J. (2002). Attitude 101.what every leader needs to know. Nashville, TN: Thomas Nelson, Inc.

Maxwell, J. (2007). *The 21 most powerful minutes in a leader's day: Revitalize your spirit and empower your leadership.* Nashville, TN: Thomas Nelson, Inc.

Maxwell, J. & Parrott, L. (2005*).* *25 Ways to win with people – How to make others feel like a million bucks.* Nashville, TN: Thomas Nelson, Inc.

Middleton, K. & Petitt, E. (2007). *Who cares? Improving schools through relationships and customer service.* Tucson, AZ: Wheatmark

Milliken, W.E. (2007). *The last dropout: Stop the epidemic!* Carlsbad, CA: Hay House.

Noddings, N. (1988, December 7). Schools face crisis in caring. *Education Week*, 32.

Payne, R. (2005*).* *A framework for understanding poverty.* Highlands, TX: aha Process, Inc.

Perfect Apology. (n.d.) *The art of apology.* Retrieved November 19, 2009 from http://www.perfectapology.com/apologizing.html

Performance Learning System. (2002). *Humor in the classroom.* Project TEACH: Teacher Effectiveness and Classroom Handling. Retrieved September 21, 2009 from http://www.plsweb.com/resources/newsletters/enews_archives/18/2002/03/07

Peterson, R. & Karschnik (2008, July 1). Communication factors. *iSpeak.* Retrieved September 12, 2009 from http://www.ispeak.com.news.asp?newsid=9

Quaglia Institute for Aspirations (2008). *My voice student report.* Portland, ME: Quaglia Institute. Retrieved January 14, 2010 from www.qisa.org.

Ramsey, R. (2008) *Don't teach the canaries not to sing. Creating a school culture that boosts achievement.* Thousand Oaks, CA: Corwin Press & National Association of Secondary School Principals.

Reeves, D. (2008, September). The extracurricular advantage. *Educational Leadership*, 86-87.

Ridnouer, K. (2006). *Managing your classroom with heart a guide for nurturing adolescent learners.* Alexandria, VA: Association for Supervision and Curriculum Development

Roeser, R., Midgley, C., Urdan, T. (1996). Perceptions of the school psychological environment and early adolescents' psycholpogical and behavioral functioning in school: The mediating role of goals and belonging. *Journal of Educational Psychology*, 408-422.

Scherer, M. (2008, September). Ode to positive teachers. *Educational Leadership*, 7.

Schmoker, M. (2006). *Results now. How we can achieve unprecedented improvements in teaching and learning.* Alexandria, VA: Association for Supervision and Curriculum Development

Schonert-Reichl, K. (2006, Feburary 16). *Pedagogical caring and students' social-emotional and academic success: The importance of teachers* [PowerPoint Slides] Retrieved July 15, 2008 from HTTP://bctf.ca/uploadedFiles/News.../**Schonert-Reichl**Presentation.pd

Schultz, J. & Cook-Sather, A. (Ed). (2001). *In our own words students' perspectives on school.* Lanham, MD: Rowman and Littlefield.

Smith, R. & Lambert, M. (2008, September). Assuming the best. *Educational Leadership*, 16-20.

Stanger, N. (2003). *Diamonds in the dew an appalachian experience.* Bloomington, IN: 1st Books Publisher.

Stiggins, R. (2007). Assessment for learning: An essential foundation of productive instruction. In D. Reeves (Ed.), *Ahead of the curve. The power of assessment to transform teaching and learning* (pp. 59-76). Bloomington, IN: Solution Tree

Stiggins, R., Arter, J., Chappuis, S., & Chappius J. (2004). *Classroom assessment for student learning: Doing it right-using it well.* Portland, OR: ETS Assessment Training Institute.

Sullo, B. (2007). *Activating the desire to learn.* Alexandria, VA: Association for Supervision and Curriculum Development.

Tileston, D. & Darling, S. (2008). *Why culture counts, Teaching children of poverty.* Bloomington, IN: Solution Tree Press.

Thompson, S., Greer, J, & Greer, B. (2004, Summer). Highly qualified for successful teaching: characteristics every teacher should possess. *Essays in Education*. Retrieved December 10, 2009 from www.usca.edu/essays/vol102004/thompson.pdf

Vatterott, C. (2009). *Rethinking homework best practices that support diverse needs.* Alexandria: VA: Association for Supervision and Curriculum Development.

Wagner, T., Kegan, R. et al (2006). *Change leadership: A practical guide to transforming our schools.* San Francisco, CA: Jossey-Bass.

Wang, M., Haertel, G.,, & Walberg, H. (2004, January; 2003, December). What helps students Learn? *Educational Leadership,* 74-79.

Weber, M. (2007, April 9). *The Importance of Interpersonal Relationships.* Retrieved October 12, 2009 from the Connexions Web site: http://cnx.org/content/m14428/1.1/

Wentzel, K. (2003, Autumn). Motivating Students to Behave in Socially Competent Ways. *Theory Into Practice,* 319-326.

Wimberly, G. (2002). *School relationships foster success for African American students. An ACT policy report.* Retrieved October 12, 2009 from www.act.org/research/policymakers/pdf/**school**_relation.pdf

Wong, H. & Wong, R. (2001). *The first days of school – How to be an effective teacher.* Mountain View, Ca: Harry K. Wong Publications.

Zapf, S. . (2008, September). Reaching the fragile student. *Educational Leadership*, 66-70.

P.S. – A Final Note

Simply the Best

Simply the Best was written primarily for teachers and administrators. However, many of the ideas shared are appropriate for anyone working with kids. Everyone in the school who interacts with students needs to know what matters to them. Most of the ideas from relationships around a moral imperative and relationships around recovery would be applicable to all school staff including office professionals, food service workers, custodians, school nurses, paraprofessionals, and bus drivers. In addition, other fields may find some of the comments from students valuable. Colleges and universities, churches, youth organizations, athletic or extracurricular program sponsors can utilize some of the ideas to foster positive and supporting relationships with children and youth.

Check It Out

If your school is interested in how to improve customer service in your organization, you may want to investigate the resource, *Who Cares? Improving Public Schools Through Relationships and Customer Service.*

A Word from Some of Our Previous Readers

- The book's intentional focus on customer service, relationships, and making connections will not only positively impact the culture of your school, but will also result in improved academic achievement. The research and practices of building relationships have been described as the linchpin to changing the negative direction characterizing so many public schools. Anyone who really cares about students will take the time to read *Who Cares?*   *Book Review* by Tonia Hopson, Pike County, KY Schools

- *Who Cares?* offers hope with real world, customer service examples and practices that have been implemented in one public school district in the battle to win back students.
  -Hotline, Publication of Kentucky School Administrators Organization

- Recently I enjoyed reading your book, *Who Cares?* Great Job! In fact, I think that the information in your book is so relevant, that my staff will receive their copy tomorrow as a Christmas present. My intent is to follow the lead of a colleague and lead other staff members through a study over the next few months to discover how we can hone in on our strategic plans….Your book is very well crafted with relevant techniques and I am really looking forward to our staff's future discussion with your book guiding us.
  -Dr. Bill Cowling, Assistant Superintendent, Blue Springs, Missouri Schools

A Snapshot of Reactions of Attendees
From Customer Service Presentations

- Dear Kelly,

  I want to thank you for coming to Keokuk. Not a day has gone by without me hearing a reference to the presentation. I ordered some additional books for those who were absent. It was an amazing couple of hours…

  -Lora, Superintendent, Keokuk, Iowa Schools

- I honestly believe that your presentation provided more merit than ANY presentation that I have ever attended in work, school, or church.

  -Chris Wilding, Upper Arlington, Ohio Board of Education

- Hi Kelly,

  I just wanted to thank you for coming to our OKSPRA meeting. I have been hearing great reviews from your presentation. You have truly made a difference in the customer service that Oklahoma students and parents will be receiving. Here are just a few of the comments:

  - One of the junior high principals who came with Amber to the December meeting was so "wowed" by our speaker that she purchased extra books to share with her faculty, initiated mini-training seminars and implemented the ideas of greeting others by name and speaking in complete sentences at her school for the month of January. Thank you, thank you for making this possible. I'm especially excited because it's happening at the junior high my son attends.
  - Thank you! Thank you! Thank you! The workshop was a turning point for our district, I believe. It has completely changed the game for many of our principals. They are sharing customer service ideas with one another. I'm having a hard time keeping up with all they want to do!

    Robin, OKSPRA, Oklahoma City, Oklahoma

Visit the following website for additional information, including training and customer service resources for schools:

www.kellymiddleton.com

Notes